RANIERO CANTALAMESSA

# THE MYSTERY OF CHRISTMAS

A comment on the *Magnificat, Gloria, Nunc Dimittis*

**THE LITURGICAL PRESS**
Collegeville, Minnesota

Cover design by Robert F. McGovern.

Original title: *Il mistero del Natale.*
© Editrice Ancora Milano, Italy, 1987.

Translated by Frances Lonergan.

English translation © St Paul Publications, Slough, England, 1988. This edition
for the United States of America and Canada published by The Liturgical Press,
Collegeville, Minnesota.

1    2    3    4    5    6    7    8    9

**Library of Congress Cataloging in Publication Data**

Cantalamessa, Raniero.
    [Mistero del Natale. English]
    The mystery of Christmas : a comment on the Magnificat, Gloria,
Nunc dimittis / Raniero Cantalamessa ; [translated by Frances
Lonergan].
        p.  cm.
    Translation of: Il mistero del Natale.
    Includes bibliographical references.
    ISBN 0-8146-1813-8
    1. Magnificat—Meditations.  2. Gloria in excelsis Deo—
Meditations.  3. Nunc dimittis—Meditations.  4. Christmas—
Meditations.  I. Title.
BS2595.4.C368  1988                                89-37971
226.4'06—dc20                                      CIP

# CONTENTS

CHRIST "A LIGHT FOR THE GENTILES AND GLORY TO HIS PEOPLE ISRAEL"

# "MY SOUL PROCLAIMS THE GREATNESS OF THE LORD"

## The mystery of the Annunciation

### Introduction to the Gospel canticles

In these meditations we are going to contemplate the mysteries relating to the birth and infancy of Jesus through the canticles in the Gospel according to Luke. We shall contemplate the mysteries of the Annunciation and Visitation in Mary's canticle (the *Magnificat*), the mystery of Christmas in the canticle of the angels (the *Gloria in excelsis Deo*) and the mystery of the Presentation in the Temple in Simeon's canticle (the *Nunc Dimittis*). In the Gospels of the infancy of Jesus these canticles are there to explain what came about in a spiritual way, that is, to enhance the meaning of the events in words, making them a form of confession of faith and praise. They stress the hidden meaning of the events which must be brought to light. As such, they are an integral part of the historic narration and not just interludes or separate passages, because every historic event is made up of two factors: the event and the meaning of the event. They give the liturgy its place in history. It has been written that "the Christian Liturgy begins with the canticles of the story of the infancy."[1] In other words, these canticles

---

1. H. Schürmann, *Das Lukasevangelium*, I, Freiburg i.B. 1982.

contain the Christmas liturgy in an embryonic stage. They are the fulfilment of the essential element of the liturgy which is a joyful celebration of belief in the event of salvation. St. Augustine explains that history tells us what happened and how it happened while the liturgy prevents the past events from becoming "past," that is, over, no longer present with us and this is done not by performing them again but by celebrating them.[2] The Gospels of the infancy also contain a "historic" account of the events that took place once and forever *(semel)*, never to be repeated again, and they also contain a celebration in canticle, thanks to which these events will be celebrated by the Church yearly *(quotannis)* in the Christmas liturgy and daily *(quotidie)* in that of the Mass and the Hours. Through the liturgy we constantly live the events in the Spirit; it makes "today" that day *(hodie)* so that in all truth we can say with the Church: "*Today* Christ is born, *today* the Angels sing on earth. . . ." Thanks to the liturgy and to the living tradition of the Church we don't have to say sadly that two thousand years *separate* us from the events of salvation, but that two thousand years *unite* us to them.

It's difficult to say who these canticles can be attributed to. Almost everything about them is uncertain. Who, in fact, composed them (Mary? the Angels? Simeon? Luke himself? Did they exist before?), the sources, the structure. . . . Fortunately, we can leave all these problems to the critics who continue to study them. We don't have to wait for these obscure points to be solved to be edified by these canticles. This is not because these problems are of no importance but because there's a certainty which makes all these uncertainties less important. Luke accepted these canticles in

---

2. Cf. St. Augustine, *Sermo* 220; PL 38: 1089.

his Gospel and the Church has accepted Luke's Gospel in its Canon. These canticles are the "Word of God" inspired by the Holy Spirit. For example, the *Magnificat* is Mary's because the Holy Spirit attributed it to her and this makes it more "hers" than if she had actually written it herself! In fact, we are not really interested in whether Mary composed the *Magnificat* or not but in knowing whether she composed it under the inspiration of the Holy Spirit. Even is we were certain that Mary composed it, we wouldn't be interested in it because of this but because it is the Holy Spirit who speaks through it. There is a spiritual truth in the Scriptures that doesn't always exactly coincide with what is called the historic truth when by historic truth we mean only what can be learned through the normal channels of human research.

With this premise and these sentiments, let us now approach the first of our canticles, the *Magnificat*, seeing it first as Mary's and then as the canticle of the Church and of the soul.

*Part One*

# THE *MAGNIFICAT,*
# MARY'S CANTICLE

The *Magnificat* "celebrates" the eschatological event of the coming of the Messiah, not so much, however, in relation to the person and nature of the Messiah himself as to the unexpected and wonderful fulfilment of all the expectations and all the promises made by God. More than the person of the Savior it is the event of salvation that is at the center of attention, the *kairos,* the new epoch that was beginning. We are looking at salvation in its nascent state. In the *Magnificat* we have the irruption of salvation in history; it has kept intact throughout the centuries the astonishment and mystery of that long-awaited moment, never to be repeated, in which prophecy reached fulfilment and history took on a new course. Mary behaves like someone who sees a stone falling into a pool of water and doesn't rush to look at it closely but remains immobile, enchanted by the ripples spreading outwards towards the edge of the pool. With the coming of the Messiah, God and the world appear in a new light and Mary is the first to see God and the world in this new light. As far as the content is concerned the *Magnificat* can be defined as a new way of seeing God and a new way of looking at the world and history. I've said "as far as the content is concerned" because the words used in the *Magnificat* are the oldest of all the canticles. It is full of expressions and reminiscences from the Old Testament. It couldn't have been otherwise. The event had to be sung in the words of those who had prepared it. No original or inedited language could have achieved the same extraordinary results of concentrating so much significance into this moment. In each word there is an epoch, a saving event, a personage, a prophecy, a figure is recalled. It's a wonderful invention by the Holy Spirit to unite the figure and the reality at the same time, to proclaim at the same time an end and a beginning. The words are the same but the situation has changed. The use of ancient words to say new things is part of the mystery of Scripture. It shows that the Incarnation is both "an old and a new mystery; old where the prefiguration is concerned and new where the event is concerned." In one way the *Magnificat* sums up much of the Old Testament; in another it anticipates much of the New Testament. The evangelical beatitudes are contained in it as if they were in germ and in the first outline. Mary's canticle is a prelude to the Gospel. Like the preludes to certain operas it contains the motifs and important airs to be developed as the opera progresses.

As I have said, Mary's canticle is a new way of seeing God and the world. In the first part which embraces verses 46-50, following what has come about in her, Mary's glance is turned towards God; in the second part which embraces the remaining verses her glance is turned towards the world and history.

*A new look at God*

The first movement in the *Magnificat* is towards God; God has absolute primacy over everything else. Mary doesn't delay in answering Elizabeth's greeting, she doesn't either enter into discourse with man, but with God. She dwells on nothing in-between but fixes her mind on God. She recollects herself and immerses herself in the infinite God. An unprecedented and incomparable experience of God has been "fixed" in the *Magnificat* for all time. It is the most sublime example of the so-called numinous language. It has been observed that when the divine reality is manifested to a soul it usually produces two opposing sentiments: fear and love, awe and attraction. God shows himself as a "tremendous and fascinating mystery," tremendous in his majesty, fascinating in his goodness. When God's light first shone on him, Augustine confessed: "I trembled with love and terror" and even later on contact with God made him "shudder and burn" at the same time.[3] We find something similar in Mary's canticle, expressed biblically, through the titles used. God is seen as *Adonai* (much more meaningful than the term "Lord" we translate it with), as "God," as "Powerful" and above all as *Qadosh*, "Holy": *Holy is his name!* A word that envelopes everything in a trembling silence.

At the same time, however, this holy and powerful God is all trusting, seen as "my Savior," as being indulgent and lovable, one's "own" God, a God for his creature. The words and the titles themselves are less important than the state of soul that shines through them; what they evoke is more important than what they say. Words could contain only in a very small way what Mary experienced in her heart. We can imagine someone sinking his hand into a heap of corn and feeling it completely covered, but when he tries to take a handful of corn and lift it out, he realizes he has only managed to get hold of a few grains.

Knowledge of God provokes, as a reaction and contrast, a new and true perception and knowledge of oneself and one's own being. The self is only grasped in front of God *coram Deo:* "A herdsman, who (if possible) is a self to his

---

3. Cf. St. Augustine, *conf.* VII, 16; XI, 9.

herd, is a very small self; the same is true of a king who is a self to those under him; in the long run neither one is a self; the term of measurement is missing in both cases. But what infinite emphasis falls on the self the moment God becomes its measure!"[4] Therefore, in God's presence the soul finally knows itself in truth. This is what happens in the *Magnificat*. Mary feels "looked" upon by God; she herself enters into that look and sees herself as God sees her. And how does she see herself in this divine light? As being "small" (here "humility" means real smallness and lowness and not the virtue of humility!). She sees herself as a "servant." She sees herself as a nothing that God has deigned to look upon.

Big experiences of God all have depth and essentiality in common. Isaiah too, when he had the extraordinary vision of God's majesty and glory, immediately became aware of himself, of what he really was and exclaimed: "Woe is me! For I am lost, for I am a man of unclean lips" (Isa 6:5ff). We are dealing with the sentiment of the creature. Mary didn't confess her "impurity" because there is no impurity in her, but just the same she recognized her nothingness as a creature. We find the same experience in the life of St. Francis of Assisi. One night, his intimate companion and confident, Brother Leo, wanted to observe unnoticed how St. Francis prayed and he saw that the saint passed long hours with his face and hands raised towards heaven, repeating over and over: "Who are you, my sweet God? Who am I, vile worm and your useless servant?" Who are you? Who am I? In this twofold question lies the whole of Christian wisdom which consists in knowing God and knowing oneself. St. Augustine also prayed to God saying:

---

4. S. Kierkegaard, *The sickness unto death*, II, A, 1.

''That I may know you and that I may know myself''
*(Noverim te, noverim me).*[5] One is essential to the other: the
knowledge of God without a knowledge of self would
generate presumption and a knowledge of self without the
knowledge of God would generate desperation.

Mary's words, therefore, shed new light on the truth
of things, truth ''suppressed by injustice'' has been freed
(cf. Rom 1:18ff). Sin is impiety, St. Paul says, keeping God's
truth suppressed by injustice and consists in not glorifying
and thanking God but in confusing one's ideas and placing the creature on the same level as the Creator. Mary in-
augurates the ''mystery of piety'' which will be divinely
fulfilled in her Son. She acknowledges the infinite difference. She attributes everything to God and nothing to herself, not only in what she is but also in what she does: *He
who is mighty has done great things for me,* she says. God is
the author, the principal agent; she is only the creature
through whom God acts, even if she is a free creature who
therefore collaborates with God by placing herself at his dis-
posal and by her willingness. Mary acknowledges ''God's
power and his splendor over Israel'' (cf. Ps 68:35). She has
really restored God's power to him! She is ''full of grace''
because she is empty of herself. At a certain moment in my
life, while I was in Lourdes on a pilgrimage, I grasped this
fact so clearly that I felt compelled to pray saying: ''Hail
Mary, *empty* of yourself . . .'' instead of ''full of grace.''
Mary is the purest exaltation of grace and it is sad that this
hasn't really been acknowledged in Christianity by those
who have spoken of grace with most authority, placing it
before merit.

From this acknowledgment of God, of herself and of

---

5. St. Augustine, *Sol.* II: 1,1; PL 32, 885.

the truth, spring joy and exultation: *My spirit rejoices . . .*
the joy of truth bursting forth, joy for the divine work, a
joy of pure and gratuitous praise. What St. Augustine says
of himself and every believer is eminently true of the Mother
of God who sings the *Magnificat:* ''I praise God and in praising him I rejoice, I rejoice in his praise. Let love and praise
be gratuitous. This means loving and praising God for himself and for no other reason.''[6] Mary magnifies God for himself, even if she magnifies him for what he has done in her;
she magnifies him for her own personal experience, as do
all the great biblical worshippers. Mary's jubilation is an eschatological jubilation for God's decisive action and it is the
jubilation of the created being for being ceatures loved by
their Creator, at the service of the Holy One, of love, of
beauty, of eternity. It is the fullness of joy. If a simple visit
of divine grace was sufficient, as with B. Paschal, to make
him exclaim on that memorable night of fire: ''God of Abraham, God of Isaac, God of Jacob . . . Sentiment, joy, peace.
Joy, joy, tears of joy,'' what must the coming of God in person into the womb of the Virgin Mother have been like?
St. Bonaventure who personally experienced the transforming effects on a soul visited by God, speaks of the coming
of the Holy Spirit on Mary at the moment of the Annunciation as a fire which inflamed all of her: ''The Holy Spirit
came upon her,'' he wrote, ''like a divine fire which inflamed her mind and sanctified her flesh conferring on her
a most perfect purity. . . . Oh, if only you were able to
feel in some measure how great was the fire that descended
from heaven and how wonderful it was, what freshness it
brought. . . . If you could only hear the Virgin's jubilant

6. St. Augustine, *Enarr.* Ps 53:10; CCL 38: 653ff.

hymn. . . .''[7] Even the strictest and most exacting scientific exegesis is aware that we are dealing with words that cannot be comprehended through the normal means of philological analysis and admits that: "Whoever reads these lines is called to share in the jubilation; only the celebrating community of those who believe in Christ and those faithful to him are able to comprehend these texts."[8] It is speaking "in the Spirit" and cannot be understood if not in the Spirit. It is like a sound being transmitted through the waves of the atmosphere which cannot be heard by those under water where there are different physical laws of the transmission of sound.

## A new look at the world

As I have said, the *Magnificat* is made up of two parts. What changes between the first and the second parts is not the language used, neither is it the tone. From this point of view the canticle is an uninterrupted flow with no breaks; the verbs continue to be in the past tense narrating what God has done or, better still, what he "has started to do." Only the background of God's action has changed; from what he did "in her" we pass to what he did for the world and for history. The effects of the definitive manifestation of God and how it reflects on humanity and history are dealt with. It is like following the stone that falls into water and makes ripples which spread outwardly towards the bank. . . .

Here we have a second characteristic of evangelical wisdom, that of uniting sobriety in the way of looking at the world to the inebriation that contact with God gives, in conciliating the greatest rapture and abandonment to God with

---

7. St. Bonaventure, *Lignum vitae*, I:3.

8. H. Schürmann, *op. cit.*

the greatest critical realism towards history and man. In the second part of the *Magnificat,* after exulting in God, Mary turns her penetrating gaze on what is happening in the world. St. Paul explains this twofold attitude well, made up of ecstasy and "folly" where God is concerned, and of wise discernment where man is concerned: "For if we are beside ourselves it is for God; if we are in our right mind, it is for you" (cf. 2 Cor 5:13).

Using a series of powerful aoristic verbs, from verse 51 on, Mary describes a pulling down and a radical reversal of men's positions: he pulled down—he raised; he filled—he sent empty away. An unexpected and irreversible turn of things because it is God's work and God never changes or goes back on his word as man does. In this changeover two differnt groups emerge; on the one hand the proud-powerful-rich, on the other the humble-hungry. It is important to understand this reversal and where it started if we are not to misunderstand the whole canticle and with it the evangelical beatitudes which are anticipated here in almost the same words.

Let us look at history: what actually happened when the event Mary sung of started to be fulfilled? Was there perhaps an external social revolution through which the rich were suddenly impoverished and the hungry filled with good things? Was there, perhaps, a more just distribution of riches among the social classes? No, not really. Were the powerful really pulled down from their thrones and the humble raised high? No. Herod continued to be called "the Great" and Mary and Joseph had to flee into Egypt because of him. If what was expected was a visible, social change, history has taught us that this was not to be the case. where then did this reversal take place (because it *did* take place)? It took place in the faith! The kingdom of God manifested itself bringing about a silent but radical revolution. It is as if something had suddenly been discovered which caused an unexpected devaluation. The rich are like those who have amassed great wealth but who, on waking one morning, find themselves miserably poor because a hundred per cent devaluation had taken place overnight. On the contrary, the poor and the hungry are favored because they are ready to accept this new situation and do not fear the change it will bring about: their hearts are ready.

As I have mentioned, the reversal of things Mary sings of is similar to that proclaimed by Jesus in the Beatitudes and in the parable of the rich man. St. James addresses the rich with these words: "Weep and howl for the miseries that are coming upon you. Your riches have rotted" (Jas 5:1-2). This does not mean that in St. James' time the wealth of the rich actually rotted. The apostle is saying that something happened to make it lose all real value; a new richness was revealed: "Has not God chosen those who are poor in the world to be rich in faith and heirs to the kingdom?" (Jas 2:5). The difference now is to be rich "in faith" and rich as "heirs to the kingdom."

Mary speaks of richness and poverty starting from God; once again she speaks *coram Deo;* God, not man, is her measure. She establishes the "definitive" eschatological principle. To say therefore that we are dealing with a reversal "in faith" does not mean that it is any the less real and radical, or serious; it is infinitely more so. This is not a pattern created by the waves on the sand which the next wave will wash away. It is an eternal richness and an equally eternal poverty. Mary's own life, and precisely Christmas, give us the best picture of all of this. Let us glance at how things went in the "inn" at Bethlehem. The rich are there, distinguished in their wide cloaks, the precious rings on their fingers and their heavy side-bags. The eminent men of Galilee and Judaea and the travelling merchants are there and they are all reverently welcomed while their horses are sent to the stables. Mary and Joseph arrive and, the Evangelist notes, ''there was no room for them in the inn'' (Luke 2:7) so they had to find shelter in a stable which might have been in the inn itself or maybe it was a different stable outside the town. There is nothing of the great reversal announced by Mary. But let us look at how things are now. Where are the rich and powerful who were so satisfied that day and so revered by all? Who remembers them now? What remains of that night they passed inside in cheerfulness? They were there but ''it was as if they had never been there.'' They were truly ''sent away empty handed.'' Instead, who does not remember with emotion, who does not honor or at least know of Mary and Joseph her spouse and the child Jesus who were held in such low esteem at that time? Could a more complete or radical reversal have been given to the world, to those who believe?

In the last verse, Mary talks of the decisive action of God which explains all the rest: ''He has helped his servant Israel, in remembrance of his mercy, as he spoke to our fathers, to Abraham and to his posterity forever.'' This is a reference to the coming of the Messiah, to the fulfilment of the greatest of God's promises. It is a return to the heart of the mystery enclosed earlier on in the words: ''The Almighty has done great things for me.'' But this mystery, at first contemplated in itself, in the divine maternity, is now seen in relation to the history of salvation. This is the focal point of the canticle: the reversal of the situation between the rich and the poor is not evoked for its own sake, but as a sign and manifestation of the eschatological event of the coming of the Messiah. To understand how new those simple closing words of the *Magnificat* are we must know what the holy men of Israel expected and asked of God, prior to the coming of Christ. Fortunately, we have one of those prayers in Sir 36:1-17, a prayer ''for the liberation and rebirth of Israel,'' at the time of the Maccabees: ''Lift up thy hand . . . . Show signs anew, and work further wonders . . . hasten the day and remember the appointed time; and let the people recount thy mighty deeds . . . . Have mercy, O Lord, upon the people called by thy name, upon Israel . . . . Fulfil the prophecies spoken in thy name . . . . ''Once people begged God to show the strength of his arm; now Mary says: He has shown the strength of his arm; he was begged to do great things and now Mary says: He has done great things; he was begged to remember but now: He has remembered; to take pity on his people, and now: He has helped Israel; he was asked to fulfil the prophecies, and now: He has fulfilled the prophecies. Through a simple change in verbe tense, Mary has expressed a change of epoch, the passage from the time of expectation to the time of the actual accomplishment of the prophecies. Something similar to what takes place in a woman's heart at the moment in which, after a long and intense wait, she finally gives birth to her child, takes place in the passage from the old to the new covenant. St. Augustine said that the old covenant was ''pregnant with Christ.'' Now he has come; he is present and no longer just waiting like a child in its mother's womb. All fears change into joy and all our doubts become certainty. The *Magnificat* has an irreplaceable and beautiful role to play in the Church: that of keeping alive the feeling for the event, the wonder of the eschatological hour, of preventing that moment of the past from being forgotten and lost forever. It has the role of preserving, in so far as it is possible, the force of that unique event. Before the event there was expectancy and after it there is the memory of the event. We live in the time of the memory of the event and in some way the *Magnificat* makes this memory present in the Spirit.

*How the incarnation came about*

We have seen that the *Magnificat* is the canticle the Evangelist Luke uses to give a spiritual interpretation to the Annunciation and therefore to the mystery of the incarnation. What does Mary say in her canticle to help us understand this mystery other than that it actually happened and that the Messiah is present in the world? Is there anything in it that shows us how the incarnation took place other than the fact itself that it did take place? Is there anything to help us grasp the essence other than the existence of the event? It is in exalting God who has chosen a humble servant for the fulfilment of his plan, God who has put down the mighty and exalted the lowly, that Mary gives us a fundamental truth to help us understand the incarnation. She tells us that it came about in humility, weakness and poverty. She tells us that God chose to reveal himself by hiding himself.

Two thousand years of Gospel preaching has made us familiar with this choice which we take for granted and which was a rule of life for the saints. But to Mary it was unheard of and full of wonder. The words "He has exalted the humble!" are exclamative and full of astonishment. She was well aware of how the Messiah was expected to appear in her world, among his people, at least among the dominant classes, whilst he is here, present in the world without anybody realizing it.

Everything Mary says concerning the divine choice of the humble and poor refers back to the Old Testament both in the terminology and the ideas that were widespread among the "pious" of Israel in her time. But where the content is concerned, the reference is to something completely new. God has given a new meaning to the ideal of the poor and humble, but now he has become poor and humble himself and this is a completely different thing. It is true that, in the Gospel, the *Magnificat* comes before Bethlehem with its poverty and before the hidden life in Nazareth but this is all anticipated in God's choice of the Mother of the Messiah, in the place and the circumstances of his coming on earth. At that time there were lots of girls in Jerusalem including rich and educated daughters of the high priests. In Nazareth itself Mary knew girls of her own age who were much more in the public eye than she herself was but she, an unknown and poor child, was the one God chose. Who would ever have imagined such a thing? When something new takes place in history or in a person's life, it is the beginning that is important and surprises us as it is the beginning that is filled with novelty. Later on we grow accustomed to it as basically the situation remains the same with only a gradual evolution. The start is the decisive point. All that follows depends on it. Thus the greatest novelty is not in Christ's passion but in the Incarnation and, speaking of the Incarnation, the novelty is not in the descent from heaven to a manger but in the descent from heaven to the Virgin's womb. It is not in the choice of a poor mother to be born in but in the choice of a poor mother to be born of. In the Incarnation the paschal mystery is already *in nuce* as the theology and liturgy of the Church has always taught us, not only because the person of the Redeemer was formed in the incarnation, the redeeming divine and human person (from which the infinite value of his death derives), but also because Christmas anticipates the way this Redeemer will save his people: through poverty, humble suffering and obedience.

In this way Mary's canticle tells us something important of the mystery of the incarnation which no metaphysical reflection on the nature of the Redeemer (one person, two natures, exchange of the idioms) could have told us. The *Magnificat* helps us to complete the essential and ontological picture of the incarnation with a more existential and religious one. It is not only important to know that God became man; it is also important to know what kind of man he became. From this point of view the *Magnificat* continues in the New Testament, in St. Paul's letters, where it is said that it pleased God to save those who believe through the folly of what is preached, that God chose what is weak in the world to shame the strong, and what is low and despised in the world, even things that are not, to bring to nothing things that are (cf. 1 Cor 1:21ff). We must have the courage to openly admit that a too unilateral and sometimes even obsessive insistence on the metaphysical aspects and problems of the incarnation has in certain places and times in Christianity caused the true nature of the mystery to be lost from sight, reducing it (as happened with the Eucharistic transubstantiation) to a metaphysical mystery more than a religious one, a mystery to be technically formulated into ever stricter categories inaccessible to people in an atmosphere of perpetual theological conflict between the different schools of ideas. St. Francis of Assisi is at truest and deepest when dealing with this matter. For him it was not only a question of the rediscovery of the importance of Christ's humanity (this had been dealt with in the battle against Docetism and Gnosticism) and not even of simple devotion to Christ's humanity (a devotion started by St. Bernard) but of a rediscovery of the *humility* and *poverty* of the

Savior's humanity. The Franciscan sources report that two things were able to move St. Francis to tears whenever he heard them mentioned: "the humility of the Incarnation and the charity of the passion."[9] At Greccio he was not moved because he saw the Son of God reduced to a tender baby, but because he saw him deprived of everything and exposed to every discomfort.[10] There is no trace here of the sentimental devotion which was later to be characteristic of the devotion to the Child Jesus. St. Francis' devotion is in line with that of the *Magnificat*, the Beatitudes and St. Paul.

The *Magnificat* does not only throw light on God's ways and the mystery of the Incarnation, but also, and above all, on Mary herself. The surest way of knowing a person intimately is through their way of praying. No one is ever so truthful and really himself as when he closes himself in his room and prays to the Father in secret. We are always conditioned when speaking with others or in the presence of others. Sometimes even out of charity and duty, we cannot be completely open and even if we wanted to we would not be able to. The very opposite happens with God: we would not be able to hide anything, even if we wanted to.

Therefore, the *Magnificat* is, above all, a wonderful window which illuminates the soul of the Mother of God and through which we can glimpse something of the splendor of the grace and wisdom with which she is filled. She is totally transparent to God. Playing on the twofold meaning of "grace," divine and human, passive and active, it has been said that Mary is "full of grace because she is full of grace" (C. Péguy). God delights in her because she is

---

9. Celano, *Vita prima*, 30.
10. *Ib.*

beautiful and she is beautiful because God delights in her; she is full of grace for everyone because God filled her with grace. Through her prayer, we see her as "the greatest queen because she is the humblest of creatures." She is nothing (in her own eyes!) but a poor servant; she is happy just being one of her own people; she reverently names Abraham, Israel and "our fathers," considering herself so small and insignificant before them whereas she is (in God's eyes!) the greatest of all creatures, the "fixed term of eternal counsel," as Dante says.

*Part Two*

# THE MAGNIFICAT,
# CANTICLE OF THE CHURCH

Commenting on the Annunciation, St. Irenaeus says that "Mary, full of exultation, prophetically exclaimed in the name of the Church: *My soul magnifies the Lord.* . . ."[11] The *Magnificat* is, therefore, not only Mary's canticle, but the canticle of the whole Church. Mary is like the soloist who starts a tune that must then be taken up by the choir. Tradition is quite convinced of this; Origen embraces it too: "It is for them (for those who believe) that Mary magnifies the Lord."[12] He too, referring to the *Magnificat*, speaks of "a prophecy made by Mary."[13] This explains the expression "Mary, model of the Church" *(typus Ecclesiae)*, used by the Fathers and acknowledged by Vatican Council II (LG 63). To say that Mary is "the model of the Church" means that she is the personification of the Church, the perceptible representation of a spiritual reality; it means that she is the model of the Church in the sense that the idea of the Church is perfectly realized first of all in her person and at the same time she is its principal member, its root and its heart.

The "choral" or ecclesiastical characteristic of the *Magnificat* is not only based on tradition; it is not just an interpretation by the Fathers of the Church but it is inherent in the

---

11. St. Irenaeus, *Adv. Haer.* III, 10:2; SCh 211, p. 118.
12. Origen, *In Luc.* VII; GCS 35, p. 54.
13. *Ib.* VII, 1.

text itself as we can see in the Bible. Mary does not speak for herself only. In the references to the Old Testament re-echoed in the Virgin's canticle, it is the "daughter of Sion" who is speaking, that is, a person representing the whole people (cf. Isa 61:10).

But what meaning does "Church" have here and in the place of which Church does Irenaeus say Mary sang the *Magnificat?* Not in the place of the nominal Church, but of the real Church, that is, not of the Church in abstract, but of the actual Church, of the persons and souls who make up the Church. The Fathers affirmed the principle by which what is said of the Church in the Scripture in a general sense is true for each soul in a singular way; *Ecclesia vel anima.*[14] "The same wisdom of God, which is the Word of the Father, universally attributes to the Church *(universaliter)* what is said especially of Mary *(specialiter)* and individually of the soul *(singulariter)*."[15] The *Magnificat* is not only to be recited but to be lived. Each one of us should make it our own; it is "our" canticle. When we say: "*My* soul magnifies the Lord," the "my" should have a direct reference. St. Ambrose wrote: "May Mary's soul be in you to exult in God. . . . If it is true that one only is the Mother of Christ according to the flesh, all souls generate Christ in the faith because each believer accepts in himself the Word of God."[16] The Church must make Mary's canticle its own for a deep objective reason: because the Church too is, in a different way, "virgin and Mother," the Almighty has done great things also in it. The Church generates Christ as well: Mary is its head, a member of the body of Christ, and if the

---

14. Cf. St. Ambrose, *De virginibus,* I, 31; PL 16:208.
15. Isaac of Stella, *Sermo* 51; PL 194:1865.
16. St. Ambrose, *In Luc.* II, 26; CC 14, p. 42.

Church "gives birth to the members of Christ, this signifies that it is very like Mary *(Maria simillima)*."[17]

In the light of these principles let us now try to apply Mary's canticle to ourselves, to the Church and soul, to learn what we must do to "be like" Mary not only in words but also in deeds. The *Magnificat* teaches us essentially two things: to be fervent with God and critical, or realistic, with ourselves and others. It teaches us a "sober inebriation of the Spirit": inebriation in the first part where God is concerned and sobriety in the second part where the world is concerned.

### Spiritual inebriation in prayer

In her canticle, Mary urges us not to be afraid of "giving ourselves enthusiastically" to God; she reminds the Church that its first impulse must always be towards God, that it must exist and talk in God's presence more than in man's presence *(coram Deo)*, even before existing for the world; it must exist and talk in God's presence more than in man's presence. She urges us to revive the ideal of spiritual inebriation in the Church, an ideal that was so dear to the Fathers of the fourth century. "The Holy Spirit," St. Augustine wrote, "has come to dwell in you. . . . He found you empty and he filled you; hungry and he nourished you; thirsty and he inebriated you. May it be only the Holy Spirit that inebriates you. The Apostle says: "Do not get drunk with wine, for that is debauchery." And almost as if to impress on us what we should be inebriated with he adds: "But be filled with the Spirit, addressing one another in psalms and hymns and spiritual songs, singing and making melody to the Lord with all your heart" (Eph 5:18ff).

---

17. St. Augustine, *Sermo Mor. Guelf.* 1:8; PLS 2:541.

Is not he who rejoices in the Lord and exultantly sings to him perhaps like one who is inebriated? I rejoice in this inebriation![18] Both real and spiritual inebriation has the same effect on us. Both draw us out of ourselves but while real inebriation makes us live beneath our dignity on the level of irrational animals, spiritual inebriation helps us to live above our dignity on a divine level. While real inebriation caused by drink, drugs or even one's own beauty, success or intelligence, makes us stagger and unstable, spiritual inebriation unites us with God and makes us stable and firm.

The *Magnificat* helps us to rediscover the beauty of pure praise, of adoring wonder before God's majesty and holiness. It urges us to recollect ourselves and lose our soul in the infinite which is God. It urges us not to content ourselves with the simple and meaningless prayer of beginners but to tend towards a "certain spiritual contact" with the living reality of God. Sometimes it is more useful to form our own prayer in close imitation of Mary in her canticle and not to limit ourselves always to repeating words we know and have learnt from others. Mary is a master at using the ancient words of the Bible to sing a completely new, fresh, spontaneous and personal prayer. The words of the *Magnificat* are full of ardent longing for God. Mary really adores God "in spirit and in truth."

Within the precise and strict frame of the liturgy it must also be possible to let the sense of jubilation that the real presence of God gives us be noticed if only through the tone of voice and the intimate participation of the heart. From the way and tone in which both the priest and people incite one another at the introduction to the preface of the Mass to praise and give thanks to God always and every-

---

18. St. Augustine, *Sermo* 225; PL 38:1098.

where, something of the spirit animating the *Magnificat* can be obvious. It would be strange if, at the priest's invitation: "Lift up your hearts," the people were to answer: "We lift them up to the Lord" *(Habemus ad Dominum)*, without ever really worrying about lifting them up to the Lord. At certain points, where the liturgy allows it, it is a good thing to break our stereotyped patterns of prayer and enliven it with a few spontaneous interventions suggested by the Holy Spirit at the moment. This could be done at the introduction and during the short admonitions preceding certain parts of the Mass and especially during the Prayer of the Faithful. It does not always have to exclusively be a prayer of petition. It could be an acclamation of praise, of thanksgiving, of jubilation and adoration with the people participating chorally, repeating at each invocation: "We praise (or thank) you, Lord!" or "How great you are, Lord!", "You are holy, Lord!", "We magnify you, Lord!"

## The Magnificat, *a school of evangelical conversion*

In the second part, where Mary proclaims the putting down of the powerful and proud, the *Magnificat* reminds the Church of the essential message it must announce to the world. It teaches the Church to be "prophetic." The Church lives and practices the Virgin's canticle when it repeats with Mary: He has put down the mighty from their thrones, the rich he has sent empty away! The Church repeats this with faith, making a distinction between it and all the other announcements it also has the right to make concerning justice, peace, and the social order in so far as it is the qualified interpreter of the natural law and the guardian of Christ's commandment on fraternal love. The Church must announce this by direct mandate as the "good news" which does not have to wait for a hypothetical universal justice to be established to be true because it is already true and already established whereas the right to announce other things is derived. The one is a free gift of God connected to the coming of the kingdom while the other is the result of man's efforts and good will. To confuse the two announcements would be to invalidate both of them and make them ineffectual by secularizing the one and sacralizing the other.

If the two views are distinct, they are not, however, separate and without reciprocal influence. On the contrary, the proclamation of faith of what God *has done* in the history of salvation (the view of the *Magnificat*) becomes the best indication of what man in his turn *must do* in his own personal history, and, rather, of what the Church itself must do on account of the charity it must show to the rich, in view of their salvation. More than ''an incitement to pull down the powerful from their thrones to exalt those of low degree,'' the *Magnificat* is a healthy warning addressed to the rich and powerful about the tremendous risk they run just as the parable of the rich man will later on be in the intentions of Jesus.

The *Magnificat* is not therefore the only way of facing the problem which is very much felt today of wealth and poverty, of hunger and having too much; there are other legitimate ways which come to us from history, and not from faith, and to which Christians rightly give their support and the Church its discernment. But the evangelical way must be proclaimed by the Church always and to all men as its specific mandate and through which it must support the common efforts of all men of good will. It is always universally valid and relevant. If by chance a time and place existed in which there was no longer any injustice or social inequality among men, but everyone was rich and satisfied, the Church would still have to proclaim, as Mary did, that God has sent the rich away empty. Actually, it would have to proclaim it with even greater energy. The *Magnificat* is just as relevant in rich countries as in countries of the Third World. There are plans and aspects of life which can be grasped only with the help of a special light, the bare eye is not sufficient; we need infra-red or ultra-violet rays. The image this special light gives is very different and surprising to those who are used to seeing the same phenomena in a natural light. Thanks to the word of God, the Church has a different image of the world situation, the only lasting image, because it is obtained with the light of God and it is the image God himself has. The Church cannot keep this image hidden. It must spread it untiringly, make it known to all men because their eternal destiny is at stake. It is the image that will remain when the "pattern of this world" has passed. At times it must make it known through simple, direct and prophetic words, like those Mary used; in the way we express things we are intimately and serenely persuaded of. This must be done even at the cost of appearing ingenuous and cut off from this world according to the prevailing opinion and spirit of the time. The Apocalypse gives us an example of this direct and bold prophetic language in which divine truth is opposed to human opinion: "You say ('you' could equally be the individual or a whole society): I am rich, I have prospered and I need nothing! not knowing that you are wretched, pitiable, poor, blind and naked" (Rev 3:17). Think of the well-known story in which some swindlers made a king believe that there was some beautiful material which would make those wearing it invisible to the foolish and stupid, and visible only to the wise. First of all the king himself does not see it but he is afraid to say so in case he is considered one of the foolish and all his ministers and his people behave in the same way. So almost completely nude the king parades through the streets and everyone, so as not to betray themselves, pretend to admire his beautiful robes until a child's voice is heard in the crowd: "But the king has got nothing on!", thus breaking the spell and everyone finally has the courage to admit that the famous robes do not exist. The Church must be like that child's voice. To a world infatuated with its own prosperity and which considers those who show they do not believe in it, it repeats the words of the Apocalypse: "you do not know that you are naked!" This shows us that Mary really "speaks prophetically for the Church" in the *Magnificat*: starting from God, she was the first to lay "bare" the great poverty of the riches of this world.

However, to limit the part of the *Magnificat* about the proud and the humble, the rich and the hungry to what the Church and believers must preach to the world would be to misunderstand it completely. We are not just dealing with something that must be preached but which, above all, must be practiced. Mary can proclaim the beatitude of the humble and poor because she herself is humble and poor. The reversal she talks about must take place especially in the heart of whoever says the *Magnificat* and prays through it. Mary says: God has scattered the proud "in the imagination of their hearts." Unexpectedly the subject shifts from outside to inside, from theological discussions in which everyone is right to the thoughts of the heart in which everyone is wrong. The man who lives "for himself," whose god is his own "self" and not the Lord is a man who has built himself a throne on which he sits dictating laws to others. Now, Mary says, God has put those down from their thrones; he has laid bare their lack of truth and injustice. There is an interior world made up of thoughts, will, desires and passions, which, St. James says, cause the wars and fightings, the injustice and abuse which are among you (cf. Jas 4:1) and while no one tries to change this situation from the root, nothing will really change in the world and if something changes it is only to reproduce, in a short time, the same situation as before.

How closely then are we touched by Mary's canticle, how deeply it scrutinizes us and how radically it "cuts the roots!" How stupid and incoherent I would be if, everyday, at Vespers, I were to repeat with Mary that God "cast the mighty from their thrones" while in the meantime I continued to hanker after power, a higher place, promotion, a better career and lost my peace of mind if I didn't succeed; if everyday I were to proclaim with Mary that God "sends the rich away empty" and in the meantime I hankered tirelessly after riches and possessions and ever more refined things; if I were to prefer being empty-handed before God to being empty-handed before the world. How stupid I would be if I were to continue saying with Mary that God "raises the lowly," that he is near to them while he keeps the proud and rich at a distance, and then did the very opposite. "Everyday," Luther wrote in commenting on the *Magnificat*, "we see that all men aim too high, at positions of honor, power, wealth, dominion, a more comfortable life, at anything which gives them importance. And we all like to be friends with such people; we run after them, serve them willingly, share in their greatness. No one wants to look down lower where there is poverty, disgrace, need, affliction and anguish. Rather, we turn our eyes away from such things. We shun and avoid those who are troubled and abandon them to themselves. No one thinks of helping or assisting them or of doing anything to help them become something; they must remain of low degree and be despised." Mary says that God does the opposite; he keeps the proud distant and raises to himself the humble and unimportant; he stays more willingly with the needy and hungry who harass him with supplications and requests than with the rich and satisfied who do not need him and ask nothing of him. Thus, with maternal tenderness, Mary exhorts us to imitate God and make his choice ours. She teaches us God's ways. The *Magnificat* is truly a wonderful school of evangelical wisdom. A school of continuous conversion. Like all the Scripture, it is a mirror (cf. Jas 1:23) and we know that a mirror can be used in two very different ways. It can be used focusing it outwards, on others, as a burning glass projecting the light of the sun on to a distant point until it causes a fire to start, as Archimedes did with the Roman ships, or it can be used keeping it focused on ourselves to see our own faces so as to remedy the faults and defects. This is the way St. James exhorts us to use it, to "get ourselves into focus" before we think of others.

St. Gregory the Great said that Scripture "grows through reading."[19] The same is true of the *Magnificat*; the words are enriched and time does not detract from their meaning. Ranks of saints or simple believers prayed with these words before we did, savoring the truth they contain, putting the contents into practice. Through the communion of saints in the Mystical Body, the whole of this immense heritage now adheres to the *Magnificat*. This is the way it should be recited, in chorus with all the worshippers of the Church. This is the way God takes delight in it. To be part of this chorus which has developed throughout the centuries, all we have to do is want to represent to God the sen-

---

19. *Mor.* 20:1; PL 76:135.

timents and transport of Mary who was the first to sing it "in the name of the Church," of the scholars who commented on it, of the musicians who set it to music with faith, of the pious and the humble of heart who lived it. Thanks to this wonderful canticle, Mary continues to magnify the Lord for all generations. Her voice, like that of a coryphaeus, supports and carries along with her that of the Church. A worshipper of the psalter invites us all to join him in saying: "Magnify the Lord with me, and let us exalt his name together" (Ps 34:3). Mary repeats the same words to us, her children: Magnify the Lord with me! "Come, O sons, listen to me, I will teach you the fear of the Lord" *(ibid.).* Mary, the Mother of the Lord, the model of the holy Church, carries the Church along with her in praising God, towards the joy of salvation; she draws it towards God. Let us say: Yes, Mother, we magnify the Lord with you and for you, for the great things the Almighty has done in you and for the great things he has also done for us. Forever and ever.

# "GLORY TO GOD
AND PEACE TO ALL MEN"

---

## The mystery of Christ's birth

Also the event of the Savior's *birth*, like that of the *Incarnation*, has its canticle in Luke's Gospel, the *Glory to God*, sung by the Angels on Christmas night. As I previously said, the canticles represent the beginning of the Christmas liturgy in so far as they are a joyous celebration, in the Spirit, of Christ's birth and infancy. For this reason they have been part of the Christian liturgy since the beginning and still play a very relevant part in it: the *Benedictus*, the *Magnificat* and the *Nunc Dimittis* in the liturgy of the Hours, in Lauds, Vespers and Compline respectively, and the *Gloria*, actually inserted into the Eucharistic Liturgy. As early as the second century, certain acclamations to God were soon added to the short canticle of the Angels (Luke 2:14): ("We praise you, we bless you . . .") which were part of the Hebrew liturgy and the New Testament. These were later followed by invocations to Christ ("Lord God, Lamb of God . . .") and, in the sixth century, the text thus extended was inserted into the Christmas Mass and other festive Masses where it has been kept as the "Great doxology."

The *Gloria*, sung or recited at the beginning of the Mass, is a recall to Christmas inserted into the very heart of the mystery of the Last Supper to signify the continuity between the birth and death of Christ, between Christmas and Easter inside the same mystery of salvation. St. Augustine distinguished in his time two ways of celebrating an event of the history of salvation, that is, by celebrating the event as a mystery or just as an anniversary.

In celebrating the anniversary, all that is required, he said, is "to indicate with religious solemnity the day of the year that recalls when the event took place." In celebrating the mystery ("in sacrament"), not only is the event commemorated but it is done in such a way as to make its significance clear and it is accepted in holiness. He considered Easter a mysteric celebration while he placed Christmas among the anniversary celebrations.[20] He said this because Christmas had not long been inserted into the Church festivities and its rich and mysteric meaning had not been closely studied. We can no longer keep this distinction today. The Christmas we celebrate is not only a "memory" but a "mystery" whose significance we must understand, welcome with holiness and imitate. A few years after Augustine's death, St. Leo the Great stressed the mysteric significance of Christmas saying that "the children of the Church were generated with Christ at his birth just as they were crucified with him in his passion and given life with him in his resurrection."[21]

*Glory, peace and benevolence:*
*the content of the canticle*

The angelic acclamation is made up of two parts in which the single terms form a perfect parallelism:

> *Glory to God in the highest, and on earth peace among men*
> *with whom he is pleased.*

---

20. St. Augustine, *Epist.* 55:1.2.
21. *Sermo* VI, 2; PL 54:213.

The twofold parallels are: glory-peace, to God-to men, in the highest-on earth. The most important thing to note about the Angels' hymn in its entirety is that "it is not really a doxology but a proclamation in the key of a hymn of exaltation. We are dealing with an expression of confession and praise, not of desire, and must be integrated with 'is' and not with 'be' ''[22]: Glory *is* to God . . . , peace *is* on earth. It is a proclamation in the indicative, not in the operative. In other words, in their song the Angels are expressing the meaning of what has taken place; they are declaring that the birth of the Child fulfils God's glory and brings peace for all men. Just as Simeon says at the moment of the Presentation: "This Child is set for the fall and rising of many" (cf. Luke 2:34), so the Angels say: "This Child is here for the glory of God and for peace, the peace of all men." The canticle of the *Gloria* is, therefore, a kind of *didascalia* placed above the Christmas scene revealing its deep meaning in a prophetic key.

Let us now try to grasp the meaning of the single terms of the canticle.

*Gloria (doxa)* does not just indicate the divine splendor which is part of its very nature but also, and even more so, the glory manifested in God's work which creates a sense of "glorification" in his creatures. We are not dealing with the objective glory of God which is always present independent of any acknowledgement but with men's knowledge or praise of the glory of God. St. Paul speaks about the "knowledge of the glory of God in the face of Christ" (2 Cor 4:6).

"Peace" *(eirene)* in its full biblical meaning denotes all the messianic promises expected for the eschatological era,

---

22. H. Schürmann, *Lukasevangelium,* Freiburg i.B. 1982.

particularly the forgiveness of sins and the gift of God's spirit. The term is quite close to that of "grace" *(charis)*, often associated with it in greetings (cf. Rom 1:7). It signifies much more than the absence or abolition of wars and human contrasts. It denotes a re-established, pacific and filial relationship with God, that is, in a word, salvation. "Since we are justified by faith," the Apostle says, "we have peace with God" (Rom 5:1). On these lines, peace is identified with the very person of Christ: "For he is our peace" (Eph 2:14). In Christmas there is already the essence of Easter because we are dealing with the beginning and end of the same mystery. Christmas represents salvation in its nascent state.

Finally, the term "good will" *(eudokia)* denotes the source of all these blessings and the reasons for God's actions, which is love. The Vulgate literally translated *"bonae voluntatis"* as "good will," meaning the good will of men, or men of good will and in this sense the expression became part of the Christian language. But this interpretation is wrong and is acknowledged as such today. The findings at Qumran made it finally clear that the genitive *eudokias* has an objective and not a subjective meaning. "Men, or children of benevolence," are said at Qumran to be the children of light, the followers of the sect.[23] We are dealing then in our canticle with men whom God loves and who are the object of divine benevolence.

In the passage from the meaning of the Qumran to that of our canticle, the gap that exists between law and the Gospel is clear. Among the Essenes the divine good will discriminates and separates certain men, distinguishing them from others. It is a genitive partitive: the men of divine good will are a chosen few. In Luke's Gospel there

---

23. Cf. *Hymns*, I QH, IV, 32 ff; XI, 9.

is nothing that authorizes us to make a genitive partitive of *eudokias* distinguishing the predestined, the object of God's free and gracious choice. On the contrary, as the Angels told the shepherds, "this joy is for all the people" (Luke 2:10) and, shortly after, Simeon will greet the Child as a "light for the people" and his salvation as "prepared in the presence of all peoples" (cf. Luke 2:21ff). St. Paul says that God desires all men to be saved (cf. 2 Tim 2:4). The fact that at Qumran the divine good will was seen in a restricted sense is of no importance as many things which were seen in a restricted sense among the Essenes and in the Old Testament, as, for example, the category of neighbors, are seen in a universal sense in the Gospel. The men of divine benevolence are, therefore, all men. When we say "man born of woman" we do not mean that a man or some men were born of woman and others were not. We are only defining man on the basis of how he comes into the world. If peace were granted to men for their "good will," then it would certainly be limited to a few as only a few deserve it, but as it is granted by God's good will, through grace, it is offered to all men.

*Christmas: the feast of God's goodness*

The key-word to the angelic proclamation is therefore the last word of the hymn. The whole unfathomable mystery of God's "good will" is contained in it. Christmas is not an appeal to man's good will but a glorious announcement of God's good will towards man. He destined us to be his sons "according to the *purpose* of his will"; "he has made known to us the mystery of his will, according to his *purpose (eudokia)*" (Eph 1:5-9). Christmas is the supreme epiphany of God's love: in it was manifested God's goodness, the Apostle says, and his love for all men *(philanthropia)* (cf.

Titus 3:4). This is the "dew" which drops from the heavens at Christmas, the "sweetness" that poured down from on high.

There are two ways of showing love for another. One is in giving gifts to the beloved. This also happens between human beings. When love blossoms between two persons, they feel the need to make gifts to one another as a token of their interest and affection. That is how God loved us in the creation. The whole of creation is a gift: the being we possess is a gift, the flowers, the air, the sun, the moon, the stars, the cosmos in which the human mind loses itself . . . . "Thou dost cause the grass to grow for the cattle, and plants for man to cultivate, that he may bring forth food from the earth, and wine to gladden the heart of man and bread to strengthen man's heart" (Ps 104:14ff). But there is a much more difficult way of showing love for another and that is to suffer for the beloved, like God's love for us in his Incarnation. "As the immensity of God's love for us was not to be hidden and in order to let us experience his great love and show us that his love for us is infinite, God invented his own annihilation, he carried it out and found the way to undertake great and terrible sufferings. Thus, because of all he underwent, God convinced man of his great love for him and drew him to himself again, man who had fled from the good Lord believing the Lord hated him."[24] He invented his own annihilation," he "emptied" himself *(ekenosen)*, and took the form of a servant (cf. Phil 2:7). God did not content himself with loving us with charitable love but he also loved us with suffering love.

We would need to have a saint's heart to understand the mystery of Christmas. The saints did not just dwell on

---

24. N. Cabasilas, *Life in Christ*, VI, 2; PG 150:645.

the surface meaning of Christmas: they went deeply into its mystery. "The incarnation," one of them wrote, "accomplishes two things in us: it fills us with love and makes us certain of our salvation. Love that cannot be comprehended! Love above which there is no greater love: my God became flesh to make me God! Consuming love: you unmade yourself to make me. The depths of your becoming man wring such passionate words for me. When you, Jesus, make me understand that you were born for me, how full of glory is such an understanding."[25] During the festivities of the Christmas in which she departed from this world, this unsurpassed scrutineer of God's depths addressing her spiritual sons who were gathered round her, exclaimed: "The Word became flesh!" And after a long hour in which she was absorbed in this thought, as if returning from far away, she added: "Every creature is overpowered. All the intelligence of the Angels is not sufficient!" And when those present asked her by what every creature was overpowered and what the intelligence of the Angels was not sufficient for, she answered: "to understand!"[26]

## Cur Deus homo?: *Why did God become man?*

In its brevity and simplicity the canticle of the Angels "Glory to God and peace to all men" helps us to find an answer based on God's Word to the ancient question of why God became man: *Cur Deus homo?* Throughout the centuries of Christianity two fundamental answers have been given to this question: one gives prime importance to the salvation of man and the other gives prime importance to God's glory;

25. B. Angela of Foligno, *Il libro*, Quaracchi 1985, p. 712ff.
26. *Ib.* p. 726.

one stresses, to use the words of the canticle, "peace to all men" and the other stresses "glory to God." The first one to be formulated was that stressing salvation. "For us men and for our salvation," says the symbol of faith, "he came down from heaven, by the power of the Holy Spirit he became incarnate of the Virgin Mary, and was made man." Depending on the environment and need created by heresy this important answer took on several shades of meaning. In an epoch in which the faith was engaged in defending the actual humanity of the Savior against Gnostics, the principle of salvation by assumption was insisted on: God saved man by taking him to himself. He saved the body by taking on a body; he saved the soul by taking on a soul; he save the will and liberty by taking on a human will and liberty. "What has not been taken on," the Fathers of the time said, "has not been healed."[27] Another answer which appeals to salvation is that of *deification* or exchange: God became man to deify man; he took on our humanity to give us, in exchange, his divinity. This is what Irenaeus, Athanasius, Gregory of Nazianzus, Maximus the Confessor and many others said.

At a certain point in the development of the faith in mediaeval times another answer to the *Cur Deus homo* came out which shifted the emphasis from man and his sin to God and his glory. This was quite a legitimate and healthy deepening of the faith, a coherent development of the dogma. Could the coming of Christ, who is called "the firstborn of all creation" (Col 1:15), depend completely on man's sin which is present as a consequence of creation. God who is "being" in himself cannot but "act" also for himself; action, in fact, follows being. St. Anselm had already followed

---

27. St. Gregory Nazianzen, *Ep.* 101; PG 37:181.

this new line in his theory on atonement. Indeed, he started
with the idea of God's honor, offended by sin, which must
be atoned for and with the concept of God's "justice" which
is "satisfied" thanks to the incarnation of the Word. He
wrote a treatise as *Cur Deus Homo?* and said: "The restora-
tion of human nature could not have come about if man
had not been able to pay God what he owed him for sin.
But the debt was so great that in order to atone for it, and
as only man was obliged to do this but only God could do
it, that man had to be God. Therefore it was necessary for
God to take a man's nature in the unity of one person so
that he who should have paid the debt and could not by
his own nature would be personally identical to him who
could pay it."[28] The situation—wrote Cabasilas, basing himself on an opinion of St. John Chrysostom—was this: according to justice man should have taken on the debt and
gained victory, but he was the servant of those he should
have defeated in battle; on the contrary, God, who could
win, was in nobody's debt at all. Man, therefore, should
have gained victory over Satan but only God could. And
then came the Incarnation, that wonder of divine wisdom:
he who should have fought and he who could win were
united in the same person, in Christ who is both God and
man, and salvation took place.[29]

Based on this new line of thought, Scotus takes a decisive step forward releasing the incarnation from its essential bond with the sin of man and making God's glory its
primary motive. The reason for the incarnation lies in fact
that God wanted someone to love him supremely and in
a way worthy of him, outside himself. "In the first place,"

---

28. St. Anselm, *Cur Deus Homo?* II, 18.
29. Cabasilas, *op. cit.* 1:5; PG 150:313; cf. St. John Chrysostom, *De resurr.*
3ff, PG 50:438.

Scotus wrote, "God loves himself; in the second place he loves himself through others who are different to him and this is pure love; in the third place he wants to be loved by another outside himself who can love him in a supreme way."[30] Christ would have become incarnate even if Adam had not sinned because he is the crowning point of creation itself; he is God's supreme work.[31]

The problem of why God became man became the object of the most passionate dispute in the history of Catholic theology. On the one hand the Thomists, the followers of St. Thomas Aquinas, upheld that redemption from sin was the main reason of the incarnation; on the other hand the Scotists, the followers of Duns Scotus, upheld that God's glory was the main reason. Today, we are no longer interested in these ancient disputes and the question: "Why did God become man?" is raised almost only out of historical interest. It is true that these disputes were exaggerated. This was due to the fact that the theology of the time was too speculative with the result that theologians sometimes wanted to know "more than it is licit to know instead of acquiring knowledge soberly," as happened when man wanted to know what would have been the outcome if Adam had not sinned. But stripped of all exaggeration, the question is too important to be left pending or allowed to sink into oblivion. The accuser, he who continuously accuses man before God and God before man, also finds a motive in theological disputes to sew together accusations against God in the heart of man. The characteristic of satanic thought, which insinuates itself ever more openly into the heart of man today, is to play on the very fine thread

---

30. Scotus, *Op. paris*, III, 7:4.
31. Cf. *Ib.*

which separates the slope of divine truths from the opposing ones of supreme falsehood, to sew together a system taking a thread from one side and one from the other side so as to confuse divine intuition and subtle blasphemy. Satan therefore throws "suspicion" even on the incarnation, saying that, all told, God did everything for himself and that he was the one to gain from the coming of his Son on earth. First of all, he procured for himself a new glory which he had not possessed before the event: that of having a divine adorer outside himself, one who would love him supremely and render him glory worthy of him. Secondly, God the Father acquired a new power over the Son. The Son, in fact, having become man is subject to the Father (as if what the Father had wanted was to have mastery over the Son!). Luther was right in saying that the objections of theologians are laughable when compared to what the devil can stir up.[32]

The essential point, therefore, of the problem facing us is this: in becoming flesh God was acting for himself or for us; was he acting out of interest or of love? The clear answer that emerges from the Word of God is that the incarnation was for God's glory, but this glory consists in nothing other than in loving man. St. Irenaeus said that "God's glory is living man,"[33] that is, that man may live and be saved. Christian piety also understood this bond between God's glory and our salvation, when, developing the angelic canticle, it prays saying: "We give you thanks for your great glory" (*Gratias agimus tibi propter magnam gloriam tuam*). Why render *thanks* to God for his *glory* if not because we understand that this glory is also in our favor? When we,

32. Cf. *Tischreden*, n. 518.
33. *Adv. Haer.* IV, 20:7.

who are evil, act "for ourselves" we do so out of the greatest egoism but then God, who is love, "acts for himself" he must do so out of the greatest love. Therefore, there are not two different motives or two motives in contrast with one another as to why God became man. There is only one motive which involves, in different ways, both God and man. God's glory consists in giving what man receives as salvation. In his Gospel, St. John also stresses this new and disturbing concept of God's glory. He sees God's supreme glory in the death of Jesus on the cross because the cross reveals God's supreme love. The glory of a God who is love cannot consist in anything other than in loving. Love and not redemption from sin is the ultimate "why" of the incarnation. We see it in the interpretation of Christ's death. At first the faith affirms the fact: "he died, he was raised," then we discover *why* he died and was raised: "for us," "for our sins," "for our justification" (cf. 1 Cor 15:3-4; Rom 4:25); finally we discover why he died for our sins: Christ "loves us and (for this) he has freed us from our sins by his blood" (Rev 1:6). What is said of his death must also be said of his birth: God loves us and for this he became man for our salvation." God so loved the world that he gave his only Son, that whoever believes in him should not perish . . ." (John 3:16). He so loved the world and for this he gave his Son!

### Someone to love in a supreme way

The medieval scholars, St. Anselm and Scotus, tended, more or less explicitly, to this harmony between God's glory and man's salvation from sin. However, their theory could not satisfy everyone as it was impeded by a theological concept of God, which, from a certain point of view, depended more on Greek philosophy than on the Bible. Together with the many reasons for preoccupation in the present-day theology of the Church there is a ferment of new ways of thinking which could renew theological ideas and bring us back closer to the Bible and to the spiritual experience of God's people. Let us see how the rediscovery of the true countenance of the God of the Bible in today's theology together with the disregarding of certain traits inherited from the "God of philosophers," can help us discover the core of truth enclosed in the ideas of the medieval scholars and especially in the ideas of Scotus, so that we can nourish our faith and the jubilation of Christmas.

In his answer to the question: why did God become man? St. Anselm started from the concept of atonement to God's justice. But, apart from the possible influence of the Germanic feudal society of the time and of the Roman law, it is certain that he was influenced by what still remained of the Greek concept of God. It has been written of this concept that "God is experienced in the unshakeable law of being, as justice *(dike)* and supreme principle of compensation. The idea of God is strictly linked with the concept of cosmic justice. Justice is the essence of this God to whom, strictly speaking, it is impossible to pray."[34] On this view of God is based the Greek tragedy in which God is the one who intervenes with divine punishment to re-establish order which has been disturbed by evil. Aristotle also saw God as being "essentially the ultimate and sufficient condition for the existence of cosmic order."[35]

The Bible also contains the idea of "God's justice" and often insists on it. But there is a fundamental difference: God's justice in the Bible and especially in the New Testa-

---

34. H. Kleinknecht, *Th. W.N.T.* III, p. 71ff.
35. *Ib.* p. 74.

ment and in St. Paul's letters, does not so much point out the act by which God re-establishes a moral order disturbed by sin by punishing the transgressors, as, rather, the act by which God communicates to man his justice, that is, he makes man just. Atonement or expiation for sin is not the condition for God's pardon, but the consequence. Finally, St. Anselm successfully strives to show the compatibility and harmony that exists between his idea of justice and that of mercy. "God's mercy," he wrote, "which might have seemed denied to you while we were deepening our knowledge of divine justice and man's sin, now appears so great and in harmony with justice that it could not be thought of as greater or most just. In fact, what behavior could be more merciful than that of the Father who says to the sinner condemned to eternal torment and who does not possess what could save him: 'Take my only Son and offer him for yourself,' while the Son, in his turn says: 'Take and be saved' "[36] Therefore God's justice does not contradict his love; it is a fact, however, that the starting point and basis of this explanation is God's justice and *honor* and not his *love*. The idea itself of justice changes when seen in a God who is above all love, as the New Testament shows us. The justice of the biblical God comes from love and not vice versa. He does not defend his justice, he grants it; he is "the Lord-our-righteousness" (Jer 23:6).

Also in Scotus' answer the drawback and even the possibility of that terrible objection we have glimpsed depend on the fact that he starts from an idea of God which is more Aristotelian than biblical. Once we get rid of this obstacle, we can see how it edifies and enriches the faith with new light instead of compromising it. Scotus said that God

36. *Cur Deus Homo?* II, 20.

decreed his Son's incarnation to have someone outside himself to love him supremely. But the fact that God "be loved" is important and is actually the only possibility for Aristotle and Greek philosophy but not for the Bible. In the Bible the most important thing is that God "loves us" and loved us first (cf. 1 John 4:10-19). "God," said Aristotle, "moves the world in so far as he is loved."[37] "The idea of a divinity whose deepest essence is love, love for man and not just for a chosen few, was not part of Greek philosophy."[38] Therefore, for as long as the dominant idea of "a God to be loved" was predominant in theology over the idea of "a God who loves," a satisfactory answer could not be given to the question of why God became man. Today, renewed contact with biblical thought and the overcoming of certain rigid scholastic metaphysics help us, perhaps, to a better understanding of certain aspects of revelation which have remained obscure, at least in theological thought, if not in the liturgy and in life. A great theologian of today wrote: "The world must know that the revelation of a God-love disturbs all that it had conceived of divinity."[39] On this point he quotes Origen: "In this love for man, the Impassible God has suffered a passion of mercy."[40] Another theologian gives the same opinion: "It is a question of a decisive turning point in our view of God who is not, primarily, absolute power but absolute love and whose sovereignty is not manifested in keeping what belongs to him for himself, but in abandoning it."[41] The sovereignty and glory of this God

---

37. *Metaph.* XII, 7:1072b.
38. E. Rohde, *Die Religion der Griechen,* 1931, p. 38.
39. H. De Lubac, *Histoire et esprit,* Paris 1950.
40. *Tom. in Mat.* 10:23; GCS, 10, p. 33.
41. H.U. von Balthasar, *Mysterium paschale,* I, 4.

are manifested "in inventing his own annihilation," in becoming incarnate for our salvation and in dying for us.

The premise leads to a new solution to the problem of God's suffering and the reason for the incarnation. God wanted the incarnation of his Son, not so much to have someone outside himself to love him in a way that would be worthy of him, as to have someone outside himself *to love* in a way that would be worthy of him, that is, without limit! This was the reason for the incarnation. Thus "corrected" in the light of the true biblical idea of God, Scotus' opinion, and that of many who came after him, reveals its fulness of newness and truth. At Christmas, when the child Jesus was born in Bethlehem, God the Father had someone to love outside the Trinity in a supreme and infinite way, because Jesus is man and God at the same time. God is defined as *Agape* in the Bible (cf. 1 John 4:10) and not as *Eros;* his love is a love of donation, not of seeking. But as Jesus says "there is greater joy in giving than in receiving" (cf. Acts 20:35), so there is greater joy in loving than in receiving love.

Christmas is not therefore only the festivity of the joy of man; it is also the festivity of God's joy. St. Leo the Great, in his vibrating sermon which we read in the liturgy on Christmas night said: "May the saint rejoice, may the sinner rejoice. . . ."[42] Yes, but may God the Father rejoice too! May the Lord rejoice because his works have reached fulfilment. All men have acquired a new splendor before God because his Son came among them who "reflects the glory of God and bears the very stamp of his nature, upholding the universe by his word of power" (cf. Heb 1:3).

The sun has shone on creation. The same difference,

---

42. *Sermo I in Nativitate Domini,* 1; PL 54:191.

or rather an infinitely greater difference, that exists between a mountain view seen by night when all is dark and frightening and the same view seen at dawn when the sun lights up the colors of the peaks and fills the valley with light, exists for God between the universe seen before and after the coming of Christ. He is the sun that "rises from on high." When the liturgy placed Christmas day on December 25, which is the day dedicated to the "invincible sun," it wanted to affirm that Christ is the spiritual sun of the world, the "sun of justice." God has no longer to ask: "On whom shall I look?" (cf. Isa 66:2); now there is a point in the universe where the Father can look and find all his pleasure. Who can tell what the new life that appeared in the poverty of Bethlehem, that child whimpering in the manger, caused in God the Father and in the whole of the Trinity? The birth of Christ is not just an event confined to history; it affects eternity. Something took place in the Trinity when the Word became flesh. The artists of the Renaissance grasped a true and deep aspect of the mystery when they depicted Christ's Nativity on terracotta. They showed the heavenly Father, surrounded by angels, enraptured before the Child lying in the manger, with the same intimate joy with which his Mother contemplates him on her knees before him. God's pleasure which is lavished on all men at Christmas is an overflow of the infinite pleasure which the Father finds in that Child and which makes him exclaim: "Thou art my beloved Son; with thee I am well pleased" (Luke 3:22). We are beloved in the Beloved; sons in the Son: "He chose us in him . . . according to the purpose *(eudokia)* of his will, to the praise of his glorious grace" (Eph 1:4ff).

*"Be imitators of God"*

Only when we have contemplated God's "good will" towards us can we deal with man's "good will," that is, with our answer to the Christmas mystery. We must express our good will by imitating the mystery of God's way of acting. The imitation lies in this: God made his glory consist in loving us, in renouncing his glory for love: we must do the same. "Be imitators of God as beloved children," the Apostle exhorts, "and walk in love" (Eph 5:1ff). God found his glory not so much in being loved as in loving and loving us first. Let us repeat with St. Francis of Assisi: "That I may not seek so much to be loved as to love, to be consoled as to console, to be understood as to understand . . . ." God, we have seen, was not content to love us with a charitable love but he loved us also with a suffering love. The day arrives for everyone when it is no longer enough to *give* but it becomes necessary to *forgive*; it is not longer enough to give presents but it becomes necessary to suffer for the loved one and for the choice made. This happens in marriage, in celibacy and in the consecrated life. What at the beginning was a spontaneous, joyful and effortless gift, becomes, at a certain point, a heavy burden or temptation, and total self-denial is necessary if we are to remain faithful to our promise. It is then that we can see if we know how to imitate God . . . .

To imitate the mystery we are celebrating means to abandon all thought of self-justice, every memory of wrongs done to us, to cancel from our hearts every feeling of resentment, even if it is just, towards everyone. It means not to voluntarily allow ourselves "hostile" thoughts against anyone: neither against those near us nor those far away, neither against the weak nor the strong, the humble nor the great, against no creature in the world. We must do this to honor the Christmas of the Lord because God did not bear grudges or look at the wrongs received, and he did not wait for others to make the first move towards him. If it is not always possible for us to behave like this the whole year through, let us do so at least when we are preparing for Christmas and in the time after it, as the fast most indicated for Advent: fast from hostile thoughts and words. There is no better way to express our gratitude to God than by imitating him.

We saw at the beginning that the *Glory to God* is not the expression of a desire or a vow but that it is a fact; it must be completed with the verb "is," not with the verb "be." However, we can and must also make it a desire and a prayer. Actually, it could be the Christmas way of nourishing prayer of the heart, which is repeated at length and says everything in very few words. The words "Glory to God in the highest" contain the best prayer of praise, and the words "peace on earth to those loved by the Lord" contain the best prayer of intercession. Repeating it in this way, we praise and intercede with words that God himself gave us through the angels. In the evangelical canticle, thanks to the Holy Spirit who inspired it and who also works in us when we are listening to it or meditating upon it, the event is present, history becomes liturgy. *Here and now,* therefore, *Peace to those he loves!* is proclaimed and it is proclaimed to *us* on God's part. May this sweet announcement reach the whole world from the inner sanctum of the Church for which it was destined: *Peace on earth to those loved by the Lord.*

# CHRIST, "A LIGHT FOR THE GENTILES AND GLORY TO HIS PEOPLE ISRAEL"

## *The mystery of the Presentation*

The Christmas revelation of Jesus continues and, in a certain way, reaches its culminating point in the mystery of the Presentation in the Temple. In this case too, St. Luke explains the mysteric significance of the event through a canticle he attributes to the aged Simeon, the *Nunc Dimittis* (Luke 2:29-32).

In the evangelical narration the rite of the presentation of Jesus immediately appears different from the usual one and very special. The terms are tacitly inverted: instead of man presenting a child to God, in this unique case it is God that presents a child to man through his prophet. God "brings the first-born into the world" (Heb 1:6). Before the rite of the Presentation and the redemption of the first-born, which is not described even if it did take place, we have the new rite in which Simeon, "moved by the Holy Spirit," takes the child Jesus in his arms and presents him to the world with his canticle in which he calls him a "light for the nations and glory to his people Israel." The *Magnificat* sings the event of the coming of the Messiah from the mother's point of view as the fulfilment of the promises and the beginning of a new world; the *Gloria* enables us to glance at the significance and reason for this event; it answers the

question: Why did God become man?; the *Nunc Dimittis*
now contemplates the Savior himself. It does not place the
*fact* that the Savior is born at the center of our attention and
not even the *reason* for which he was born, but the *person*
who is born. In a few simple words something of incalcul-
able importance is proclaimed: the birth of this child has
a determining significance for the whole of humanity; it goes
beyond the boundaries of Israel. It is before him that the
decision on who is saved and who is not saved it taken.

The canticle is composed of two movements or parts:
a subjective or personal part in which Simeon expresses his
sentiments and state of mind in the presence of the awaited
Messiah, and an objective and universal part in which he
talks of the Messiah as ''a light for the people and glory
to his people Israel.'' We shall begin our reflection on the
second part which directly concerns Christ because, even
if it comes later in the order of presentation, it comes first
in the order of things and all the rest depends on it. We
shall first read the *Nunc Dimittis* in a christological and ecclesiastical light and then in a personal one. We shall apply the ancient principle of spiritual exegesis: *Ecclesia vel
anima,* according to which ''what is said in the Scriptures
of the Church in general is true for each single soul.''[43]

---

43. Cf. St. Ambrose, *De Virginibus,* I, 31; PL 16:208.

# Part One

# THE *NUNC DIMITTIS*
# IN AN ECCLESIAL READING

In St. Luke's Gospel, in which the Temple has such an important part, the coming of Jesus to the Temple is the meeting-point between the Law and the Gospel, between the old and the new covenant, between the old and the new temple. Now the prophecy of Haggai on the glory of the new temple built after the exile has been fulfilled: "The latter splendor of this house shall be greater than the former" (Hag 2:9). Old Simeon, who takes the child Jesus into his arms and asks to be allowed to depart this world in peace now that he has fulfilled his duty, has always been seen as a plastic symbol of the Old Testament who announces and awaits the coming of the New Testament and who, once this has appeared in the world, does not disappear but simply stands aside as John the Baptist did when he said: "This joy of mine is now full. He must increase and I must decrease" (John 3:29-30). In presenting the child as "a light to the people" Simeon was recalling the prophecy on the Servant of the Lord of whom it had twice been said that he would be "a light to the nations" (cf. Isa 42:6; 49:6). The time of prophecy has ended and the time of fulfilment has started. The barycenter and character of prophecy itself changes with Simeon, as it had done with Mary in the *Magnificat*. It is no longer a question of announcing future things, referred to the last days, as it had been for Isaiah and all the Old Testament, so much as acknowledging the presence of a person, of recognizing and announcing, in the

Spirit, Christ present in the world which is the whole meaning of Christian prophecy.

The figurative meaning (as the fulfilment of the prophecy) of the Presentation in the Temple has always been emphasized by the liturgy which saw in it the fulfilment of Malachi's prophecy: "And the Lord whom you seek will suddenly come to his temple; the messenger of the covenant in whom you delight" (Mal 3:1). In commenting on this episode St. Ambrose said: "Here you can see how the sequence of events of the Old Law was an image of the future."[44] However, the episode of the Presentation does not just underline the newness of the New Testament and the gospel, it also underlines its *continuity* with the Old Testament. In the Vespers of the Byzantine liturgy for the feast of the Presentation, called *Ipapante*, the *Meeting* feast, this hymn is sung:

> You, Simeon, welcome the lawmaker
> whom Moses glimpsed through the clouds,
> become a Child and obedient to the Law.
> He who had spoken through the Law,
> He who had spoken through the prophets,
> He who becomes incarnate for us
> and who saved man. Let us adore him!
>
> *(Stichira idiomela* of the Vespers)

The Presentation is truly the *Meeting* feast *(Ipapante)* and not only is it so between Simeon and Christ, but through them, between the Law and the Gospel and between the two Testaments. When commenting on the Presentation in the Temple, Origen himself, who was so sensitive to the difference between the letter and the spirit, stressed this

---

44. St. Ambrose, *In Luc.* II, 56.

vital continuity against the heretics who saw a contrast between the Old and the New Testament. With reference to Luke 2:25 he exclaimed: "Where are those who deny the God of the Law and who affirm that in the Gospels Christ revealed a different God?"[45] If, on the one hand, with all these prophetic references and the words "the glory of his people Israel," Jesus is presented to the world as the meeting-point and passage between the Old and New Testaments, on the other hand, with the words "a light for the people," he is presented as the meeting-point between Israel and the rest of humanity, as he who will break down the dividing wall and make "one new people in place of the two" (cf. Eph 2:1-14). Christ does not therefore only mark the passage from the *old* to the *new*, but also from the *particular* to the *universal*, from one people to all peoples. His salvation has been "prepared before all peoples," but this, far from diminishing the greatness of Israel, will increase it. In fact, the unique privilege of Israel will be that the Messiah, who is "its glory" will also be "a light for the nations." In a certain sense it could be said that the glory of Israel lies in the fact that Christ is the light of the nations. This means that salvation is universal in its destination but that it "comes from the Jews" (cf. John 4:22).

Seen in this light, as the Fathers of the Church and the Liturgy have always done, the episode of the Presentation of Jesus in the Temple with the spiritual interpretation Simeon's canticle gives it, is extraordinarily relevant and could be a real source of light and ecclesial discernment in the debates going on today on the significance of Christ in relation to other religions and to the Jews, that is, in the dialogue between the Church and Israel and with all

---

45. Origen, *op. cit.* XIV, 7; GCS, 35, p. 39.

peoples. The prophetic interpretation applied to the *past* becomes the springboard for an ecclesial interpretation applied to the *present.*

*Christ, a light for all peoples*

In presenting salvation which appeared in the world at Christmas, as having been "prepared before all the peoples" and the Messiah himself as a "light for the nations," Luke has already expressed the certainty of faith on the absolute and universal significance of the person of Christ which will be repeated in thousands of different ways throughout the New Testament. For example, in St. John with the words: "No one comes to the Father but by me" (John 14:6) and, "I am the light of the world" (John 8:12) and in the Acts of the Apostles with the words: "There is no other name under heaven given among men by which we must be saved" (Acts 4:12). The pagan world refused at first to take this pretence seriously and they defined it as "folly" (cf. 1 Cor 1:18ff), or "irrational."[46] Later on, in the fourth century, when Christianity was emerging victorious from the bloody combat with the pagan world, this would make a final effort at survival taking refuge in a conciliating position. One of its most illustrious leaders wrote: "there is more than one way to reach the great mystery of the Truth" (Symmachus), meaning by "one way" that of the Christians. Behind this defense of pluralism, religious relativism was, in fact, hidden: it is impossible to know God as he really is, therefore all efforts and ways to reach him are equally good and to be respected, even that of pagan Rome!

The Christian answer to this objection, given indirectly by Augustine, was that it is true that there is not only one

---

46. Cf. Celsus, in Origen, *C. Cels.* I, 9.

way to reach the truth, unless, however, the truth itself does not become the way! In this case it is no longer true that one way is not sufficient and that all ways are good; the truth, in fact, is sufficient in itself. But this is precisely what happened when "the Word was made flesh!" He, who as God was the Truth and the Life (because "in him was *life* and the life was the *light* of men"), now, as man, is also the Way and can therefore say: "I am the Way, the Truth and the Life" (John 14:6). "Dwelling with the Father, he is the Truth and the Life; on becoming flesh, he became the Way."[47] "The Life was made manifest" (1 John 1:2), that is, it became the Way!

It is around this certainty that Christ is the only divine way of salvation and that no other name has been given to man by which he can be saved, that the Christian conscience has been built and the Christian mission has developed throughout the centuries. But now the Christian conscience is in a state of crisis; it is being threatened. The certainty that Jesus is the one, only and definite way to God is losing strength. Some of the symptoms of this crisis are of a practical nature while others are of a cultural and theological nature. One symptom, or rather one given fact, is that numerous Christians from our Western world are changing over to other forms of so-called "alternative" or "substitution" religions: to Christian sects of a syncretistic nature, trends or circles of oriental spirituality, techniques of meditation which, from being mere tools, often end up as an autonomous religious "belief." The cultural and theological symptoms are more insidious as they act from within the Church where points of convergence and synthesis beyond the great Christian dogmas are sought for.

---

47. St. Augustine, *In Iob.* 34:9.

Could, for example, a meeting-point not be reached between the Christian idea of a personal God and that of the impersonal god of oriental religions (forgetting, in practice, the Trinity), between Christian Scripture and the scriptures of other religions, between Christian redemption and Buddhist liberation? A few even advance the idea of a divine economy of salvation which is greater and more comprehensive than that of the Bible and of which the world of the Bible itself is part. This all started, I believe, as a reaction to the traditional affirmation: "outside the Church there is no salvation" (*'extra Ecclesiam nulla salus'*). In part this reaction was right, since in such a context the stress was too much on the visible Church. The sad thing is that it also involved Christ with the Church, whereas the two things cannot be purely and simply confused and if we can no longer say, at least with the meaning of the past: "Outside the Church there is no salvation," we can and must say: "Outside Christ there is no salvation!"

This misunderstanding also arises on a theological level from the fact that no distinction is made between the importance of inter-religious dialogue and the importance of the profession of faith in the Church. Dialogue implies respect for the feelings, for the liberty of others, a prudent respect for the times which God also showed when revealing himself to man. But this prudent and, so to say, suspensive attitude cannot be transported exactly as it is to the profession and explanation of faith carried out in the Church without betraying the faith itself, without transforming respect for pluralism into religious relativism or, worse still, into apostasy. We cannot deny ourselves what we acknowledge for all others, that is, the right and the duty to profess to the end what we believe in.

It was the Christian mission that suffered most from this

situation of theological uncertainty. There are missionaries (fortunately, I believe, not very many) who, after all they have read in their homeland before leaving for the missions, ask themselves if Christ is, after all, the only true Way to God, if it is necessary to openly announce Christ (even where this is allowed), or if it would not be enough, instead, to promote the religious values of the people they are working for and help them to be "better Muslims" or "better Hindus," thus transforming themselves more into promoters of civilization than of the faith, and creating political consciences rather than announcing God's word.

St. Paul wrote: "There is one God, and there is one mediator between God and men, the man Christ Jesus" (1 Tim 2:5). It is the second part of this affirmation that is being challenged: the unicity of the Mediator. A similar thing happened at Colossae in the early Church. There were teachers in that city who challenged the unicity of Christ. Christ figured as one of the mediators, even if as the most important one. Side by side with him was acknowledged the autonomous power of certain angelic forces who possessed a part of the divine *pleroma*, each controlling a part of the universe or a sector of human life. In this some scholars gave way to Jewish and pagan influences; it was an attempt to introduce syncretism into the Christian faith. As soon as St. Paul learnt of this he wrote his letter to the Colossians. This is entirely a *kerygma*, that is, literally, a "cry" raised in the name of the purity of the faith. The fulness of divinity dwells only in Christ and it is in Christ alone and is not shared with any other created being. By his death he subordinated to himself and reconciled all men with God. He is, therefore, the only Savior and sufficient for everyone. Other saviors cannot exist. It is true that there are superior spirits and angelic powers in the universe who exercise a certain influence, but these have been subordi-nated to Christ and are his servants. The Apostle concludes telling us: "As, therefore, you received Christ Jesus the Lord, so live in him, rooted and built up in him and estab-lished in the faith, just as you were taught, abounding in thanksgiving. See to it that no one makes a prey of you by philosophy and empty deceit, according to human tradi-tion, according to the elemental spirits of the universe, and not according to Christ" (Col 2:6-8). Paul established the criterion for the first fundamental "discernment of the spirit" within the Church: there is only one divine way to salvation and this way is called Christ; all the others are "human ways," "elements of the universe" which do not go beyond the horizon of the universe even when they are good.

Here we are in the very heart of the apostolic *kerygma* and we can see that the unicity, universality and absolute-ness of the redemption worked by Christ is part of this heart: "For although there may be so-called gods in heaven or on earth . . . , yet for us there is one God, the Father, from whom are all things and for whom we exist, and one Lord, Jesus Christ, through whom are all things and through whom we exist" (1 Cor 8:5ff).

Yet, even then the faith could not ignore a whole reli-gious world consolidated and full of prestige. Was dialogue possible from such an "intransigent" position as that of the Gospel? Yes, it was, and the Apostle himself gives us an example in the discourse he held at the Areopagus of Athens. The discourse does not tend to belittle or throw a bad light on the religion of the Athenians, but rather it reveals its intrinsic orientation towards Christ: "What there-fore you worship as unknown, this I proclaim to you" (Acts 17:23). The Christian faith does not destroy but rather "adds truth'' to their deepest expectations and intuitions such as we "are God's offspring." What they had been seeking up to then "groping as in the dark" is now revealed in its full light in Christ. The idea that the divinity is similar to gold, silver and stone, that is, idolatry, could no longer be taken seriously and lost all conviction.

It is important for us today to note something in St. Paul's way of acting. On arriving in Athens he himself realized and recognized that the Athenians "were fearful of the gods"; which was to say, very religious (or more religious than others). He could therefore have asked himself for what reason he should disturb those people who had such a strong religious sense and such an elevated philosophy, with a new announcement so far removed from their culture. He could have said: let us leave them to their beliefs! But he did not say this; instead he held that just because that people was very religious, the crucified and risen Christ must be announced to them. A natural religious or philosophical sense and *kerygma* of faith are very different things which do not exclude each other but may even integrate.

The Fathers of the Church who came later faced the problem more directly: what should they think about the religious truth existing outside the Christian faith (for example, in Greece) and they even formulated a criterion of judgement. "Our religion," wrote Justin, "appears more sublime than any other human doctrine for this reason: because Christ, who came for us men, represents the Logos in its totality. In fact, whenever philosophers and legislators of all epochs declared or discovered something as good, they did so through investigation and intuition, according to what part of the Logos they had been granted. But as they did not know the whole of the Logos, which is Christ, they often contradicted one another. Each one of them, in fact, according to the Divine Seminal part of the Logos, expressed truths which had a certain affinity with the Logos and yet, however, they made contradictory propositions on essential points thus showing that they did not have a great scientific knowledge and indisputable learning. In fact, all the writers were only able to see the truth in an obscure way, and this thanks to the presence of a seed of Logos contained in it."[48] A constructive relationship was, therefore, set up between the Christian Truth and Greek truth, as between the *Whole* and the *parts*. But we are not dealing with a static relationship in which each side can be content with what it possesses: *the seeds of the Logos* scattered outside Christianity are waiting to be integrated into the *whole Logos* which is Christ. There is, therefore, an expectation of Christ even outside the Bible. If the Old Testament leads towards Christ as a *figure* to *reality*, Hellenism also leads towards Christ as a *part* tends, by an internal mechanism, to become part of the *whole*, just as by physical law drops of water tend to join together to form a single rivulet. This criterion is just as profoundly valid when applied today to dialogue with other religions. In fact, Vatican Council II mentions it in the decree on missionary work: Christians "must be familiar with the national and religious traditions of others, gladly and reverently laying bare the *seeds of the Word*, which lie hidden in them."[49]

It is as if an appeal were being raised to Christ from within other religions. The Acts of the Apostles tell how Christianity crossed the borders of Asia and entered Europe: "And a vision appeared to Paul in the night: a man of

---

48. II *Apol.* 10.13.
49. *Ad gentes*, 11.

Macedonia was standing beseeching him and saying: "Come over to Macedonia and help us!" And he sought to go on into Macedonia concluding that God had called him to preach the Gospel to them" (Acts 16:9ff). The same silent appeal is being raised today, if we know how to listen to it, by those who do not know the Gospel. It is not a question of their having to deny their religious values which are often high values, but of completing them. To those peoples and those cultures too, Christ, arriving among them, repeats what he said in his time of the Mosaic Law: "I have not come to abolish but to fulfil" (Matt 5:17).

Clement of Alexandria, and other Fathers with him, said that philosophy had been like an education for the Greeks which was to lead them to Christ, a sort of introduction to the faith,[50] just as in a very different way, the Law had been for the Hebrews. The founders of the various religions are sort of "forerunners" like John the Baptist. If they could talk today, they would say as he did: "I am not the Christ," and if they were asked: "Who are you then?", they would each reply: "I am the voice of one crying in the wilderness, 'make straight the way of the Lord!' " (John 1:20-23). Yes, each one of these has prepared the way of the Lord among his own people. They, too, are part of the great "evangelical preparation." If, as it is licit to think, these men have been saved and are with God, they are so through Christ's merits because "one has died for all" (2 Cor 5:14) and certainly not through their own works and knowledge.

An objective fact establishes this relationship of subordination which would otherwise be unacceptable: Jesus, and only Jesus, presented himself to men as "God" and he justified this claim in thousands of ways while other historical

---

50. Cf. *Str.* 1:5.28.

founders of religions claimed they were "masters" or "prophets," that is, "men"; their "ways" are human ones.

To make other religions preparatory ways to Christ, "human ways" that prepare the "divine Way," is not to humiliate them but, rather, to exalt them because it is not humiliating for man to subordinate himself to God. To say that Christ is "a light for the nations" is not paying honor to Christ but to the nations. Jesus said: "He who does not gather with me scatters" (Luke 11:23). All that does not lead to Christ, even very remotely, in other religions is lost because in the end only what has been summed up in Christ and "delivered by him to the Father" remains (1 Cor 15:25). It is not a question of the followers of other religions accepting this Christian point of view (this is the fruit of conversion and depends on the divine *oikonomia* of salvation and on the missionary effectiveness of the Church) but at least of it being clear and pacific to us Christians. If it is not even clear to us, how could we collaborate with the divine plan which "desires all men to be saved and to come to the knowledge of the truth" (1 Tim 2:4) which is Christ? If Christ is a light for the people, who are we to place this light "under a bushel"? On the contrary, we must place it on a candelabrum so that it gives light to everyone in the big house the world is. At the beginning of Christianity, Tertullian addressed a heretic who denied the true humanity of Christ with a heart-stricken appeal which applies also today to those who deny Christ's true divinity and the universality of salvation: "Do not destroy the only hope of the whole world: *parce unicae spei totius orbis!*"[51] Christ is the secret hope of all people and all religions which must not be destroyed.

---

51. *De car. Chr.* 5:3; CCL 2:881.

*Christ, the "glory of Israel"*

The words of the *Nunc Dimittis*, as well as throwing light on the present problem of the relationship between the Church and non-Christian religions, also throws light on the problem of the relationship between the Church and the people of Israel, between Christians and Hebrews. If Christ is "the glory of his people, Israel," we Christians must do all we can, first of all to acknowledge this ourselves and then to remove the obstacles that prevent Israel from acknowledging it. The first and most important obstacle to be removed is what St. Paul called "hostility," "the dividing wall" built on mutual incomprehension, diffidence and resentment, a wall that Jesus knocked down by his death on the cross (cf. Eph 2:14ff), but which must still be knocked down in deed, especially afer all that has taken place in the last twenty centuries since Christ's resurrection. St. Paul teaches us that the best way to a reconciliation between Israel and the Church is through love and esteem: "I am speaking the truth in Christ," he wrote to the Romans, "I am not lying; my conscience bears me witness in the Holy Spirit, that I have great sorrow and unceasing anguish in my heart. For I could wish that I myself were accursed and cut off from Christ" (Paul separated from Christ!) "for the sake of my brethren, my kinsmen by race. They are Israelites and to them belong the sonship, the glory, the covenants, the giving of the law, the worship and the promises; to them belong the Patriarchs, and of their race, according to the flesh, is the Christ" (Rom 9:1-5).

This was my own experience some years ago during my second pilgrimage to the Holy Land. The first thing I realized while still on the way there was that, as a Christian, I could not remain prisoner of the political judgements the world was passing on Israel in the atmosphere of attacks

and reprisal which had started after the Israelites had con-
quered Arab territory but that I was obliged to love this
people because "of their race, according to the flesh, is the
Christ." I should love them as Jesus, Mary, the Apostles
and the whole of the primitive Church that came from the
Jews did. It was a question of a kind of conversion to Israel
that I had never experienced before then and, like all con-
versions, it exacted a change of mentality and heart.

They, the Jews, are of the same blood as Jesus and it
has been written that "no man ever hates his own flesh"
(cf. Eph 5:29). Jesus, who is a man like us even if he is God,
is pleased if we Christians love one another and make ex-
cuses for his people even if they have not accepted him up
to now. It often happened to me in my priestly ministry
to get to know young boys and girls who were rejected and
often even ill-treated by their parents for consecrating themselves to God and I saw the joy they experienced when I
spoke well of their parents and tried to excuse them. They
were happier than if I had said they themselves were completely right and had spoken about the injustice of their
families. In the case of Jesus this is a consequence and a
nuance of his real incarnation which we must respect almost with modesty, just as we respect a family tragedy of
a friend, mentioning it with discretion and sorrow. Israel
is the first-born of God: "When Israel was a child, God
loved him" (cf. Hos 11:1) and we know that his love is "eternal" (Jer 31:3).

Christians must love Israel not only in *memory* but also
in *hope*; not only for what it was but for what it will be. Their
"fall," says the Apostle, "is not forever" and God "has
the power to graft them in again" (cf. Rom 11:11, 23). If their
rejection means the reconciliation of the world, the Apostle
continues, what will their acceptance be but life from the

dead? (cf. Rom 11:15). Simeon said that Jesus was "for the fall and resurrection of many in Israel" (Luke 2:34), which could be understood as: for the fall of *some* and the resurrection of *others* but also, as the Apostle meant: *first* for the fall and *then* for the resurrection of Israel. From the point of view of the Christian faith, all these centuries have been an extension of the wait, like a long *détour* in history, which we do not know how much longer is going to last, to arrive at when Jesus will again pass before Israel who will be able to say, as it is written. "Blessed is he who comes in the name of the Lord" (cf. Luke 13:35).

On that journey these thoughts unexpectedly gave rise to the certainty in me that the Church is responsible for Israel! It is responsible in a unique way, differently from how it is to all other people. The Church alone guards in her heart and keeps alive God's project for Israel. This responsibility of faith requires the Church to love the Jews, to wait for them, to ask, as it already does, their pardon for having in certain times hidden the true Jesus from them that Jesus who loves them and who is their "glory"; that Jesus who taught us to let ourselves be scorned and killed rather than scorn and kill others. If the delay has been so long and painful, it has also undoubtedly been so through the fault of Christians. In this light we can understand the new signs we are experiencing in the Church, such as the constitution *Nostra Aetate* of Vatican Council II, the Pope's visit to the Jewish synagogue in Rome, where he addressed the Jews as "elder brothers," and, finally, the norms emanated by Rome to eliminate from the Christian catechism and preaching all those elements and ways of expression that could offend the sensitivity of the Jews and that are not required or justified by faithfulness to the Word of God.

Together with this responsibility which is relative to the

past, there is another that concerns the present situation of Israel as a people and a state. Human and political judgements can be made on this present situation as can judgements of theology and faith. Political judgement is that expressed by heads of States and which the U.N. also expressed in its turn. There is a whole area of different and opposing opinions open here, because all political thought, including that of Israel in the Old Testament, is in itself ambiguous, mixed with man's sin even when God makes use of it for his plans of salvation, as happened in the Old Testament. The unresolved problem of the Palestinians driven out of their land makes these political judgements more of a condemnation of Israel than of approval. But, as I have already mentioned, Christians cannot stop at these political or diplomatic judgements. There is a theological or historical saving dimension of the problem which only the Church can feel. We share with the Jews the biblical certainty that God gave them the country of Canaan forever (cf. Gen 17:8; Isa 43:5; Jer 32:22; Ezek 36:24; Amos 9:14). We know, on the other hand, that "the gifts and the call of God are irrevocable" (Rom 11:29).

In other words we know that God gave Israel the land but there is no mention of his taking it back again forever. Can we Christians exclude that what is happening in our day, that is, the return of Israel to the land of its fathers, is not connected in some way, still a mystery to us, to this providential order which concerns the chosen people and which is carried out even through human error and excess as happens in the Church itself? If Israel is to enter the New Covenant one day, St. Paul tells us that they will not do so a few at a time but as an entire nation, as ever-living "roots." But if Israel is to enter as a nation, it must be a nation, it must have a land of its own, an organization and a voice in the midst of other nations of the earth. The fact that Israel has remained an ethnic unity throughout the centuries and throughout many historical upheavals is, in itself, a sign of a destiny that has not been interrupted but is waiting to be fulfilled. Many peoples have been driven out of their land over the centuries, but not one of them has been able to remain intact as a people in their new situation. Faced with this fact we cannot but remember the words of God in Jeremiah: ''If this fixed order departs from before me,'' (the order that governs the sun, the moon, the stars and the seas!) ''says the Lord, then shall the descendants of Israel cease from being a nation before me forever'' (Jer 31:36). Even the huge cross that Israel carried on its shoulders is a sign that God is preparing a ''resurrection'' for it, just as he did for his Son who represented Israel. The Jews themselves are not able to completely grasp this sign in their history because they have not completely accepted the idea that the Messiah ''should suffer these things and enter into his glory'' (Luke 24:26), but we Christians must grasp it. When Edith Stein saw the tragedy that the Nazis were preparing for her people looming up, she recollected herself in prayer one day in the chapel and afterwards wrote: ''There, beneath the cross, I understood the destiny of God's people. I thought that those who know that this is the cross of Christ are in duty bound to take it upon themselves in the name of all the others.'' And she in fact took it upon herself, in the name of all the others.

The Church must therefore keep watch over these signs as Mary kept the words in her heart and meditated on them (cf. Luke 2:19). The Church cannot go back and take on the features of the old Israel with its strong bond between race, land and faith. The new salvation has been prepared ''for all peoples.'' What is required is that the Israel according to the flesh enter into and become part of the Israel according to the Spirit without for this having to cease being Israel *also* according to the flesh which is its only prerogative. Thus St. Paul together with all those who have passed from the old to the new covenant can say: "Are they Hebrews? So am I! Are they Israelites? So am I! Are they descendants of Abraham? So am I!" The Apostle even says: "I am a better one" (cf. 2 Cor 11:22ff) and he was right, at least according to the Christian faith, because only in Christ is the destiny of the Hebrew people fulfilled and its greatness discovered. We are not saying this in a spirit of proselytism but in a spirit of conversion and obedience to the Word of God because it is certain that the rejoining of Israel with the Church will involve a rearrangement in the Church; it will mean a conversion on both sides. It will also be a rejoining of the Church with Israel.

The reconstitution of the Jewish nation is a wonderful sign and opportunity for the Church itself, the importance of which we are not yet able to grasp. Only now can Israel take up again the question on Jesus of Nazareth and, to a certain degree, small but significant, this is what is happening. Quite a few in the Jewish religion have started to acknowledge Jesus as "the glory of Israel." They openly acknowledge Jesus as the Messiah and call themselves "Messianic" Jews, which is like saying "Christians" in the original language, without bothering about the Greek translation. These help us to overcome certain gloomy prospects of ours, "making us realize that the great original schism afflicting the Church and impoverishing it is not so much the schism between East and West or between Catholics and Protestants, as the more radical one between the Church and Israel.

Sometimes in the New Testament, especially after the

resurrection, the turning to the Gentiles is spoken of as being a consequence of Israel's rejection: "Since you thrust it from you, and judge yourselves unworthy of eternal life, behold we turn to the Gentiles. For so the Lord has commanded us, saying, "I have set you to be a light for the Gentiles' " (Acts 13:46ff). But in the *Nunc Dimittis* at the beginning of the Gospel, the question is dealt with instead according to God's original and marvellous plan in terms of harmony and mutual edification which has not yet been compromised. The fact that Christ is "a light for the Gentiles" is not seen as a punishment for Israel but as its "glory." How lovely it is, in the Christmas context, to put this original view of things back into the center of the Church's attention because, in the end, this will be fulfilled as nothing and no one can prevent God's plan from being accomplished in the time established by him. One day Christ will also be, in deed, both "a light for the Gentiles and the glory of his people Israel," as he already is by right! Simeon's was not just a wish but a prophecy.

*Part Two*

# THE *NUNC DIMITTIS*
# IN A PERSONAL
# AND SPIRITUAL READING

Now we might be able to understand better the first part of Simeon's canticle which I have called the subjective or personal part. How does Simeon behave in front of the wonderful prospect he sees opening up for his people at the beginning of the new Messianic times? It is relevant and important to know this because, through Simeon's example, God's word teaches us how to behave in front of that new prospect which history is opening to the Church today. In few words Simeon gives us a fundamental lesson which is useful especially for those who hold public offices in the Church. He teaches us to be detached, free of spirit and pure of heart. He teaches us how to face with serenity that delicate moment in life when we retire from work on pension which so often becomes a drama or at least a cause of suffering and loss of peace. "Lord," said the old priest, "now lettest thou thy servant depart in peace, according to thy word . . ." (Luke 2:29). The least we can say, on reading these words, is that Simeon faced his death with serenity. He was not worried about having a part or a name in the incipient Messianic era; he was happy that God's work was being fulfilled; whether this was done with him or without him was of no importance.

The Bible introduces us to a number of these men of the *Nunc Dimittis*, men for whom God counted infinitely more than the task God had assigned to them. Moses was one of these. He went up to Mount Nebo, finally saw the Promised Land for which he had sighed and suffered and received the "command" to die from God and he died in peace (cf. Deut 34:4ff). John the Baptist was another of these "free" men. When he recognized the promised Messiah he said, almost in the same words as Simeon used: "Now my joy is complete. He must increase and I must decrease." And he accepted to die in peace without seeing the fulfilment of what he had had to announce. St. Paul is another of these men: "The time of my departure has come," he said to the disciple Timothy. "I have fought the good fight, I have finished the race, I have kept the faith. Henceforth, there is laid up for me the crown of righteousness . . ." (2 Tim 4:6-8). He said this while much of his work was still undone and much of what he had done was in danger of being lost. His glance strained forward to what lay ahead, he "pressed on toward the goal for the prize of the upward call of God. . ." (cf. Phil 3:13ff). Another man who lived the Spirit of the *Nunc Dimittis* was the martyr Ignatius of Antioch: "It is a joy," he said on his way to Rome to face martyrdom, "to die for the Lord and rise again with him . . . . It is a joy for me to die in Jesus Christ . . . . I am seeking him who died for us; I want to be with him who arose for us." He did not allow himself to be held back even by the thought of his Church which he was leaving in far-away Syria without its pastor and in such troubled times. He entrusted it to those that remained saying to them: "Remember the Church of Syria in your prayers which has God as pastor in my place. Jesus Christ and your charity will watch over it."[52]

---

52. St. Ignatius of Antioch, *To the Rom.* 2:2, 6:1, 9:1.

But why should we be satisfied with human models when we have a divine model? Jesus is the divine model of the *Nunc Dimittis*. He had just started his real and true messianic work, we might say, of healing the sick, consoling the troubled, preaching the Kingdom, when the hour arrived for him to leave everything and go alone towards his "hour." He did not think or tell the Father about all he still had to do according to prophecy, or that it might have been better for him to stay longer to strengthen his vacillating disciples or defend his reform . . . . He said: "I am coming to thee . . . I am praying for those whom thou hast given me . . . they are thine . . . I am no more in the world but they are in the world and I am coming to thee . . ." (cf. John 17:6ff).

These men of the *Nunc Dimittis* love to say to God, together with psalmist: "There is nothing upon earth that I desire besides thee. My flesh and my heart may fail, but God is the strength of my heart and my portion for ever . . . ." (Ps 73:25-26) and God loves to tell these men as he told Abraham: "I am your shield; your reward shall be very great" (Gen 15:1). This is anything but easy! But it is a "joy" to admire the summit even from a distance and with God's help set out towards it or simply desire it in the bottom of our hearts. It is a joy to go beyond half measures and become totally dazzled with the absolute. St. Teresa of Avila left us a sort of testament in the words: "Let nothing disturb you, let nothing frighten you, everything passes; only God does not change; patience wins all; he who has God is lacking in nothing; God alone suffices." God alone! These words sum up the spirit of the *Nunc Dimittis* better than any others.

The *Nunc Dimittis* is not useful only for the hour of our death or retirement from work. Even now it encourages us to live and work in this spirit, in the office we hold, in doing our duty, whether it be important or not, so as to be able to leave it with the serenity and peace of Simeon; to live in the spirit of the resurrection, a girdle round your waist, a rod in your hand and sandals on your feet, ready to open to your Lord when he comes and knocks at the door . . . .

To be able to do this we must also "take the child Jesus into our arms." With him held close to our hearts, everything is easier. Simeon faces his death with great serenity because he knows that after death he will find the same Lord and he will be with him again in a different way. "If one is leaving the world," Origen exhorts, "if he has been freed from the place of prisoners to go and reign, let him take Jesus into his arms and keep him close to his heart and then he can joyfully go where he wants."[53] There are ranks of saints in heaven who, when they were on earth, shared Simeon's privilege of holding the child Jesus in their arms. There have been too many witnesses to this in the history of the saints for it to be doubted. While one of these saints, the Blessed Angela of Foligno, particularly dear to me, was enjoying this privilege Jesus said to her: "Whoever does not know me as a child, will never know me as a man": whoever does not understand Christmas will not understand Easter, whoever does not understand the child in the crib will not understand he who is on the cross. Sometimes, to obtain some of the great graces we have caught a glimpse of in these meditations on Christmas, we could say the Rosary of the joyful mysteries with simplicity, together with those saints who held the child Jesus in their arms, to help them give thanks, to revive in the Father's heart the joy of

---

53. Origen, *In Luc.* XV; GCS, p. 103.

that moment when Someone appeared in the world whom he could love in a supreme way . . ., and ask them to help us also to hold the child Jesus to our hearts in faith and ardent devotion in the land of our pilgrimage. Let us turn to Mary, saying: "Show us *in* this exile, Jesus, the blessed fruit of thy womb, o clement, o loving, o sweet Virgin Mary!"